A Halleluiah Song!

A Halleluiah Song!

❦

Memoir of a Black Catholic Priest from the Jim Crow South

The Very Reverend William L. Norvel, S.S.J.

Cover Photo by Michael Alexander
50th Anniversary Mass
March 21, 2015, Atlanta, GA
Edited by Paulette Norvel Lewis
© The Very Rev. William L. Norvel, S.S.J.   All rights reserved 2016

ISBN: 153518292X
ISBN 13: 9781535182928

Dedication

I dedicate this book to my beloved parents, William and Velma Norvel, who were my inspiration and role models. Without their prayers, sage counsel, faithful support, and unconditional love, my journey would have undoubtable echoed a different song. They were the wind beneath my wings!

Table of Contents

ACKNOWLEDGEMENTS

"Thank You Lord"

I AM TRULY grateful to my family and for my family, the Norvel clan. It is because of their unconditional love and unfailing support that I am, who I am, and that I was able to become a priest of God.

My parents, William and Velma Norvel, were the most important and inspirational people in my life. I am profoundly grateful to them for giving me life, for sharing their wisdom, for forming my character, and for giving me loving support during good times and in challenging or difficult times. Most of all, I thank them for fostering and nourishing my faith. Next to my faith, they were God's most precious gift to me. May they rest in peace.

My sisters have been a special blessing! They have consistently provided me with their love and support and have used their talents and resources on my behalf. Kirticina ("Kirt") is sensitive, generous, and creative. Over the years, she has hemmed my pants, cooked for me, and made many beautiful Afri-centric vestments for me. I am particularly grateful to her for so generously sharing her home with me during vacations and times of transition.

Carolyn is compassionate, thoughtful, friendly, generous, and a good old fashioned cook. She, like my father, meets no strangers. My friends have easily become her friends. She is the keeper of family history, legacy, and traditions, including our mother's delicious fruit cake recipe. If my siblings and I ever need to know who in the family did what, why, and when, we call her. She is "there" for everyone and for me, in a special way.

My "baby" sister, Paulette, is creative, fun-loving, generous, a gourmet cook, a business person, teacher and editor of this autobiography. Her home has become home for all of us during holidays and special occasions. She goes out of her way to make these occasions special and memorable for our family and friends. I am deeply grateful and indebted to her.

I am also grateful to Paulette's husband, Marion. He is a great cook, musician and trainer. He has generously shared all of these talents with me. Most importantly, he is a man of strong faith. When Marion and Paulette married, I was so grateful to finally welcome another man to the family!

I am profoundly grateful to each member of my immediate family; Kirt, Carolyn, Paulette and Marion, for "having my back" and for helping to make me the person I am today.

Over the years, a number of families in the parishes I have served have helped to keep me grounded by sharing their homes and families with me. I am sincerely grateful to those who regularly invited me for Sunday dinners, included me in family celebrations, or took care of my dog, Duke, when I had to travel: Becky and Robert Scriber; David and Mary Alice James; Betty and Leroy Norton; and, my cousin, Ivrion Nelson. You not only fed my body but you also fed my spirit and my soul by supporting me in my ministry and helping to keep me grounded.

I am profoundly grateful to Sr. Marianna Halsmer, Sr. Lois Davis, Sister Patsy Guyton, Sr. Charlotte Marshall, Sr. Clementina Givens, Sister Barbara Jean LaRochester, Rose Thurston, Doris Savoy, Fred Calloway, Catherine Turner, Donna and Millicent Hawkins and the many "Mothers of the Church" in each of the parishes that I pastored. I will also always treasure the friendships of Frs. Peter Hogan, Joseph Verrett, and Kenneth Brown. (May they rest in peace.) Many others (too many to name!) supported me over the years--personally and in my many pastoral efforts. If I have failed to name you, please charge it to my head and not my heart. Know that I am grateful. All of you prayed for me, encouraged me, gave me respite and were not afraid to tell me the truth—even when it wasn't easy. Thank you!

I am grateful to those who took the time to read all or part of my memoir and provide invaluable comments: my brother-in-law, Marion, Secretary Alexis Herman, Reverend Mary Pharmer, Sister Eva Lumas, S.S.S., Rawn Harbor, Faith Cola and, of course, my sister, Paulette. May God continue to bless each of you and all that you do to bring about the "Beloved Community" of humankind.

Finally, I want to thank the Josephites for giving me the opportunity to fulfill my life's dream to become a priest and for providing me with opportunities to contribute to the African American community and the Catholic Church. I am particularly grateful for their assistance during my mother's illness.

It is my prayer that my memoir will be an inspiration to many: to the people I have been privileged to serve in priestly ministry and to young men aspiring to serve the Lord as priests. To all, I say, "Be not afraid!" Embrace your purpose and your journey with joy and dedication. In the end, the ups and downs, joys and sorrows of life form a beautiful and precious tapestry of love, inspiration, memories, and legacy. In the words of St. Augustine, "We are Easter people and 'Halleluiah' is our song!"

May St. Joseph encircle all of you in his fatherly arms of protection and love!

The Very Rev. William L. Norvel, S.S.J.

FOREWORD

꧑

"For Every Mountain"

*"How shall I make a return to the Lord for
all the good he has done for me?"*

I AM AN African American man who was born and raised on the Mississippi Gulf Coast during the late 1930's and the 1940's. I have always wanted to be a priest. When I entered the seminary, I did not know that the innocent promise of a teenage girl (my mother) to give God her first born child in exchange for her happiness, had already possibly set the course of my life journey.

I was raised as a Catholic and educated in Catholic schools. In 1965, during the height of the American Civil Rights Movement, I was ordained a priest and became a member of the Society of St. Joseph of the Sacred Heart (Josephites), a religious community whose mission, for over 144 years, has been to evangelize and serve African Americans through the celebration of the Eucharist, education, administration of the sacraments and preaching the Word of God.

My mission as a priest has been to facilitate and enhance the participation of African Americans in the Catholic Church through cultural empowerment, increased contributions to the liturgy, and the development of lay and religious leaders. It is my great fortune that this mission is in complete alignment with the mission and vision of the Josephites.

Over the years, I have been encouraged by friends and family to write my story. At age 80, I have finally had an opportunity to reflect and write. I have chosen to punctuate the content of each chapter of my memoir with the title of a gospel song or spiritual that reflects my sentiments about the experience in that chapter. These songs that speak of God's fidelity, love, and mercy, have always been a source of joy and comfort for me. They have been central to my efforts to uplift the beauty and spirituality of African American culture in the Catholic liturgy in order to provide my African American brothers and sisters with a more authentic worship experience.

My background (my upbringing, my southern roots, my Catholic faith, and growing up in the Jim Crow south) has been the motivation and inspiration for my ministry as a Josephite. It is my hope that my memoir will tell a compelling story of how these elements converged to form me as a human being and give purpose and meaning to my life. "For every mountain, he's brought me over… For every trial he's brought me through… For every blessing… For this I give Him praise!"

In the words of Langston Hughes and Maya Angelou respectively, "Life ain't been no crystal stair" but "I wouldn't take nothing for my journey now". I have had an exciting and challenging life as a priest and especially as a pastor. I hope that I have grown in wisdom, knowledge and grace. I pray that I have been able to make a positive difference in the Church, for the Josephites and in the lives of the beloved African American communities that I have had the privilege to serve.

CHAPTER 1

--------- ✂ ---------

"Bring Up a Child..."

"I Decided to Make Jesus My Choice"

I WAS BORN on October 1, 1935 in Pascagoula, Mississippi, the oldest child and only son of William ("Willie") and Velma Norvel. I have always wanted to be a Catholic priest and it has been my joy and privilege to serve the Lord as a Josephite priest for more than 50 years. This is my story....

My parents were nurturing, loving and faith-filled Christians who worked hard to shelter, educate and shield their four children from all harm including, the cruelty of cultural and systemic racism in the south.

Daddy was raised in a devout Methodist family that loved children, family and church. He was a kind, fun-loving and affectionate person. His family was the only "wealth" he needed or desired. We never doubted that he loved us dearly. He was the life-giver in the family: cheerful, fun-loving, and optimistic. He had a great sense of humor and a servant spirit. Nothing delighted him more than teasing us, Momma, or one of his many nieces or nephews. He always found time to help others, even sometimes at his own expense. He taught us to love and revere our elders. As children, and even later when we came home for holidays, he made sure we visited our elders: our aunts, uncles, older relatives, his friends, and friends of his parents. He enjoyed telling them, our neighbors and even strangers about our achievements and academic or career successes. He worked day and night in his auto-body repair shop to put bread on the table for his family all the while, whistling as he worked. His greatest gifts to us were a sense of gratitude and family pride.

1

Momma was the heart of the family and, of course, the disciplinarian. She maintained a clean and tidy home, kept food on the table and clothes on our backs. She was an excellent cook--her gumbo was "to die for" and the favorite of the entire family. Momma had a number of jobs as a domestic worker before becoming a cafeteria manager in one of the local public schools. She retired from this position after more than 20 years of service. She kept her children in school and in church and encouraged us to share the little we had with neighbors and friends. Momma took great pride in being Counselor of the Junior Daughters of the Ladies Auxiliary of the Knights of Peter Claver and the head of the Legion of Mary in the parish. She had a spirit of service to the church, friends and neighbors. She faithfully washed and ironed the church linens each week and cleaned the church when necessary. Her greatest gifts to us were nurturing a strong faith and excellence and pride in our work.

Our parents considered themselves blessed with their four children: William, Kirticina ("Kirt"), Carolyn and Paulette, all of whom were the apples of their eyes. Everyone in town knew we were Norvels and specifically, the children of Velma and Willie. We knew not to embarrass them in public and to always be on our best behavior.

We were nurtured and encouraged to succeed by the love and support of the Norvel clan, most of whom resided either in Pascagoula or Moss Point (three miles away). We grew up with five aunts, five uncles, (two of my father's siblings died at an early age) and forty-six cousins. During the early years of my youth, all lived within four blocks of one another. The youngest uncle, Harding, my father's youngest brother, took me under his wings and became my buddy. He played ball with me, took me fishing and gave me the nickname of "tadpole" (I'm not sure why.) I will never forget the time he took me fishing on the Pascagoula River without either of us getting permission from Momma or Daddy. While we were gone, a neighbor rushed to tell Mom that she saw me fall into the river and drown. Well, the heavens burst open and grief, tears and disbelief invaded our home and community! Mom was inconsolable! Shortly after the news broke of my drowning, I showed up in the car with Uncle Harding.

Seeing the crowd of people at the house, we wondered what all the commotion was about. My friends gasped in disbelief as they pointed to me and declared that I was dead! I reassured them that I was not dead but very much alive. Mom grabbed me in her loving arms and told me to "never do that again". In her joy and relief, she forgot to paddle my rear! My Aunt Delphine (Delphine Ladnier, my Mother's godmother) and Grandma Callie (my Father's mother) regarded this incident as a sign and told me that I would live a long life. That prediction turned out to be true.

We learned the dignity of work and a strong work ethic from my parents. Daddy rose each morning at 5 a.m. to light the gas heaters before going out to work in his garage auto shop. As a young man, he had worked at Ingalls Shipyard and at the United States Post Office. After serving in the military, most of his brothers, like their father, started construction-related businesses in—carpentry, masonry, plumbing, electrical. Daddy also had these skills and could repair almost anything which he did not only at home but for neighbors and friends. His first love however, was cars. Over the years, he grew increasingly tired of working in subservient positions and being looked upon as a "boy". He worked hard to perfect his skills as an auto mechanic, body and fender repair and paint professional. Eventually, he started his own business in our garage. He worked hard day and night. As a young boy, I worked with him many nights sanding and taping up cars to prepare them for painting.

Mom arose at about 7 a.m. to prepare breakfast for us before going to work as a cafeteria manager at the public school down the street from our home. During holidays, workers from other schools would come to her school for holiday meals. They knew that the meals, homemade dinner rolls, and desserts would be well prepared and delicious. When she retired, she received an award for perfect attendance during the entire 20 plus years that she worked in the public school system.

All of us had chores around the house. In addition, it was also not unusual for us to be found in the garage helping Daddy to finish a car---sanding a fender or holding the clamp as he welded a patch to the corroded area of a car, all the while being careful not to look at the intense flame emanating from the torch. Mom believed that "an idle mind is the devil's workshop". She did her best to make sure that the devil stayed far away from us.

We gathered pecans from the three trees in our yard and picked figs from the enormous tree in the back of our house. Fresh figs topped our cereal but more importantly, they were made into my Mom's delicious fig preserves. The pecans were used in cookies, candy, cakes, and Mom's delicious fruit cakes at Christmas.

When we weren't at church, school, or doing our chores, we played marbles, roller skated down the street, rode our bicycles, played with our cousins and neighbors or swung in the swing that Daddy had hung on the front pecan tree. My sister, Kirt, recalls that we also played Mass in the backyard. I was the priest, of course, and reverently distributed "communion" (Necco Wafers candy) to the girls.

On the 4th of July, my Dad and Uncle James ("Snook"), picked up all of the children and took us fishing and crabbing. When we returned home, Momma had started making gumbo and my aunts had made potato salad and coleslaw to go with fried fish. Daddy rigged up tables in the yard: paper-covered plywood on top of construction horses. All of the relatives came over, including the New Orleans clan, and a good time was had by all.

The Norvel clan gathered and shared on other holidays and whenever one of the older cousins returned to town from school or their jobs out of town. In the summer, we got strawberries and mulberries from Aunt Eudora ("Dora"); pork from Uncle "Snook" and, of course, everyone got chickens, figs and pecans from Daddy. Aunt Ella was our seamstress; her husband, Uncle Sylvanious ("Van"), provided each family with Christmas trees and turkeys; Aunt Henrietta was our nurse, and aunt "Dora" was our pre-school teacher. Aunt Alvenia ("Bena") and Mom were the cooks in the family and Aunt Georgia was the gardener and crafter. Uncle Norman, was our plumber, Uncle John was a contractor and Uncle "Snook" was a carpenter and brick mason; Uncles Harding and Frank were the electricians; and, Daddy was the mechanic. Uncle Harding was also a photographer and the first African American licensed electrician in the State of Mississippi. Almost every service needed by the family was provided within the family.

I am told that when a new grandchild was born, Grandpa Frank would gather the entire family at the home of the new parents to pray for the new baby. Every Christmas, Uncle "Snook" brought each of his young nieces and nephews a small bag containing fruit and Christmas candy. And, when any of his nieces or nephews got into trouble or needed anything, they knew to call my Dad, "Uncle Willie". Every day after school, most of the grandchildren would stop by our grandparents' home. On Easter, the dining room table was filled with brightly colored eggs--there for the taking of all of the grandchildren. Our family was not rich in material things but we were rich in love for one'another and for God.

I cherished my first job as the neighborhood paper boy, selling the local newspaper, the Chronicle Star. Every Friday, my dog, Butch, and I delivered one hundred and seventy-five papers by bicycle to clientele who were totally committed to my service. With the little profit I made, I bought a Bulova watch that had captured my attention at Johnson Brothers Jewelers.

When I grew up, life in Pascagoula offered Black children few opportunities for advancement or hope for attaining the "American dream". We could become domestic workers, barbers, teachers, undertakers, nurses or mid-wives. With the exception of domestic work, Blacks could only provide services in the Black community.

Our parents did all that they could to help us maintain our dignity, family pride and love of God. We faithfully attended and supported St. Peter the Apostle Catholic Church. The church and school provided a strong foundation and helped us to grow and mature into healthy teenagers. From this small Black Catholic community (about 250 people), six religious vocations were fostered: two priests (both Josephites, one became a bishop and I became Superior General); three religious sisters (one cloistered nun, one Superior General, and one member of the governing counsel of her order); and one religious Brother, a Josephite. The Josephite Fathers and the Sisters of the Holy Ghost affirmed our spiritual and academic potentials and prepared me and my siblings to matriculate at Our Mother of Sorrows High School in Biloxi and Most Pure Heart of Mary in Mobile, where Paulette went to high school.

Because of segregation, we could not go to the beautiful white-sand beach within walking distance from our home. If we wanted to go to the beach, we had to travel thirty-nine miles to *Mon Louis* Island, a small island outside of Mobile, AL inhabited by Creoles. When we went to the local movie theater, we had to walk up side stairs to view the movie from the "Colored" balcony. We had to enter the local department store from a back entrance and use a separate dressing room. And, of course, we drank from the "Colored only" public water fountains. Although we were aware of the discrimination, our family and church lives were so full that, as young children, we did not feel particularly deprived.

I cherished the Sundays when Mom took us to worship at St. Mark African Methodist Episcopal Church, the church of the Norvel clan. Grandpa Frank Norvel, a renowned contractor in the city, built the church in about 1925. He had the foresight to include a restriction in the deed that the church could never be sold. It still stands today in the middle of a commercial district in Pascagoula.

Grandpa Frank was a Trustee of the church and Grandma Callie helped with communion. Their daughters Ella and Eudora played piano for church services; Henrietta taught Sunday school; and other members of the family (including my Dad) sang in the choir. All thirteen of Frank and Callie's children and their grandchildren were expected to be active in the church.

What a fellowship we experienced at St. Mark! Many of the Norvels still worship there and my sisters and I are always welcomed when we return. The reason Mom occasionally worshiped at St. Mark was to nourish and strengthen her relationship with my father's family and our neighbors. Since she was raised as an only child, the Norvels were the only family she knew and she loved them dearly. At St. Mark, she was "Miss Velma" and daddy was "Mr. Willie". We were all loved and respected as Christians and as sons, daughters, and grand-children of Frank and Callie Norvel.

Oh, how I enjoyed the Methodist hymns! They never ceased to stir my youthful soul with warmth, love and faith! I still treasure and carry my Dad's Methodist Hymnal with me everywhere that I am assigned. Needless to say, I dreaded going to school on Monday mornings after attending St. Mark. I just knew that Sr. Celine would find out and give me the blues for having attended a Protestant Church on Sunday.

Over the years, I had several other jobs including working at the Veneer Mill and cleaning the home of Mr. and Mrs. Martin, owners of Pugh's Florist. Mr. and Mrs. Martin were wonderful people and devout Catholics. Mrs. Martin told Mom that I cleaned her home better than any adult. Although they were Caucasian, they were friends of our family. Until their deaths, they acknowl-edged holidays and special family occasions by sending flowers to our parents. We continue to patronize Pugh's Florist even today and the Martin children continue to acknowledge the unique relationship between our parents. I also worked sometimes as a clerk in my Aunt Delphine's general store. I waited on customers, received and stocked goods on shelves, put sodas in the "ice box" and coal in the stove, swept the floor and even counted the money before closing the store in the evening.

In order to send the four of us to St. Peter Elementary School (maintained by the Josephites and staffed by the Sisters of the Holy Ghost) and high schools in Biloxi (Sisters of the Blessed Sacrament) and Mobile (Sinsinawa Dominicans), it was necessary for both of our parents to work. Although the tuition was not much at the time, it was often a struggle for our parents to make the payments. It was a sacrifice that both of them were willing to make in order to ensure that we had a good education and a chance at a better life.

Even as a young boy, I was inspired by the commit.nent the Josephites' showed to pastoral ministry and to serving their flock. In spite of the fact that I had never seen a Colored priest, I still wanted to become a Catholic priest. Father Tom Sheedy, a jolly and fun-loving pastor, took me along with him on his many pastoral visits. Father Sheedy considered himself a part of every family in the parish. Families were delighted but never surprised when he showed up for Sunday dinner.

Father Edward Lawlor was the ideal parish administrator. He taught me the many aspects of parish administration and would sometimes send me to transact business for the parish. One of his passions was to ensure the education of the children in the parish. He financed the college education of many of his parishioners in several parishes from Birmingham, AL to Pascagoula. It was he who demolished the old wooden, two-story elementary school and replaced it with an attractive brick school equipped with a stage, cafeteria and gymnasium. All of the parishioners were very proud of it.

I graduated with good grades from St. Peter Elementary School (the old wooden structure) and prepared myself to attend Our Mother of Sorrows High School (OMS) in Biloxi, MS. Our Lady of Victory Catholic High School, only a mile from our home, would not accept Black students. So, each morning I walked past Our Lady of Victory on my way to the Greyhound Bus Station for the twenty-five mile trip (each way) to attend school in Biloxi.

My schoolmates respected my desire to be a priest; they began to call me "father" when I still was in high school. The girls affectionately called me "sweet William". When I was only a sophomore, I told my parents that I wanted to become a priest. This came as no surprise to them, they were fully aware. They told me that they would support me, but not until I had finished high school.

They felt that I needed more time to mature by socializing with my peers in high school. I was happy with their response.

I had no idea of the barriers I would encounter as a black man aspiring to become a Catholic priest in the South. At that time, there was only one seminary in the United States that would accept Black candidates: St. Augustine Seminary, the Society of the Divine Word (S.V.D.'s), in Bay St. Louis, Mississippi. Only the white S.V.D.s could be assigned in the Diocese of Jackson. At the time, the bishop of Lafayette, LA was only bishop in the country who would accept Negro priests in his diocese. One of the priests that he accepted was from Our Lady of Perpetual Help, a Josephite parish in Washington, D. C.

I spent two years at OMS High School. It offered me all that my parents hoped for: a good education and the opportunity to play basketball, attend dances and get into mischief with the other boys. The Blessed Sacrament Sisters treated me as a potential seminarian as did the Josephite pastor of OMS, Father Francis Dynan.

I loved the game of basketball. I played center on Our Mother of Sorrows' basketball team. Unfortunately, we didn't have use of a gym to practice or play in. We had to be bussed twenty miles away to St. Therese Parish in Gulfport to play games. Whenever we did have a game, Mom and Dad gave me permission to stay overnight at the home of the Marino family. This gave me the opportunity to get to know them and to share in the faith that inspired their daughter, Eileen, to become an Oblate Sister of Providence and their son, Eugene, to become a Josephite priest. Those were happy days. Father Marino later became the Vicar General of the Society of St. Joseph of the Sacred Heart (the Josephites) and the first African American Archbishop of the Archdiocese of Atlanta, GA.

Mother Mary of Mercy, the Principal of OMS High School gave us our first lesson in race relations. Although OMS students frequented a Dairy Queen a few blocks from the school, we could only be served at a side window reserved for "Colored" patrons. One day, Mother Mary of Mercy marched her students down to the Dairy Queen and informed the owner that her students would no longer patronize the store until they could be welcomed at the front window. The owner saw us as a threat to his business so, he closed the side window and began to serve us from the front window. It was my first experience of protesting the injustices that we faced on a daily basis and sometimes accepted too readily. Although we subconsciously thought "that's just the way it is," we were, at the same time, very aware that it would be dangerous to speak up.

The Blessed Sacrament Sisters were committed to educating the whole person. They often took us to New Orleans to visit Xavier University, the only black Catholic University in the United States. The university was founded by the Superior General of the Blessed Sacrament Sisters, St. Katherine Drexel. During our visit, we were able to talk with the college students, sit in classes, and visit the Pharmacy and Music Departments. It was during my visit to Xavier that I acquired a love for opera. I saw my first opera, "Carmen", at Xavier University. It was thrilling--a life-changing experience that has led to a great deal of joy over the years! To this day, I continue to listen to the weekly radio broadcasts of "Opera at the Met" and go to live performances whenever I can.

While I was still in high school, Fr. Lawlor invited me to accompany him for the episcopal ordination of Father Joseph Bowers (a S.V.D. priest from Jamaica) at St. Augustine Seminary in Bay St. Louis. Of course, I jumped at the opportunity and into the car for the ninety-minute drive. Cardinal Spellman of New York was the ordaining prelate. Many other bishops and priests from throughout the South and around the country also attended. Needless to say, this little black boy was overwhelmed by the pomp and circumstance surrounding the ordination. There were about ten Black priests, twenty seminarians, and a couple of Brothers participating in the ceremony. I had never seen so many Black priests in my life! The Catholic Church was arrayed in all of her glory! I was overwhelmed with emotion and a desire to be a part of it all.

During the ordination, I experienced my first personal encounter with Jesus, my Good Shepherd, calling me to be a priest. I have no doubt that He spoke to me that day and assured me of His loving support. As soon as I returned home, my Mom knew that something spectacular had happened to me at the ordination. I told her then that I must enter the seminary in September. She said: "You have my blessing and your father's. Just remember that the door swings in and it swings out. You can always come home."

I immediately began to compose my letter to Bishop Richard R. Gerow, Ordinary of the Diocese of Jackson, Mississippi, seeking permission to study for the priesthood in the Diocese of Jackson. I waited patiently for his response. Finally, Mom handed me the letter from Bishop Gerow. I anxiously opened it only to be shocked at his response: "There is no place in the Diocese of Jackson for a Colored priest." Needless to say, I was devastated and sunk deeply into a hole of despair and shame caused by this response from the Catholic Church that I had grown to love and wanted so desperately to serve.

Our pastor, Father Lawlor knew about the bishop's response and noticed my depression and pain. He asked me if I would like to become a Josephite. I responded immediately with an enthusiastic, "Yes". He told me to pack my bags.

Although I could never forget it, the shame caused by the earlier rejection temporarily melted away with Father Lawlor's acceptance and affirmation. The Church was full of contradictions. I thank God for those courageous and dedicated white religious men and women who worked to educate us and to demonstrate God's love for those considered "the least of these" in American society. In many ways, these men and women were the defenders of the faith. Without their examples and contributions, there would probably be fewer African Americans in the Catholic Church today.

When I told my parents of Father Lawlor's invitation, they reluctantly told me that they did not have the money to purchase a train ticket to Newburgh,

New York nor did they have money for tuition, new clothes and books. My dream was once again dashed. When I told Father Lawlor about my family's inability to pay for my trip to New York or college tuition, he assured me that he would pay all of my expenses and that I should continue to prepare to go to the seminary. People in the community bought clothes for me and gave me pocket money for travel. I will never forget the day I caught the Louisville & Nashville train, the "Humming Bird", to Newburgh, New York to begin my junior year of high school at Epiphany. Almost everyone from our parish, family and neighborhood was at the train station to see "little Willie" off to the seminary. It was exciting and a bit scary at the same time. This would be my first time away from my home and family for an extended period of time.

The Early Years

Our family in the front yard: Carolyn, me, Mom, Dad, Paulette, Kirt

St. Mark AME Church

Members of the Norvel clan gather at Aunt Ella's: I'm kneeing in front with my cousin Peter; Mom and Dad are left of me behind Peter

Me at age 12

Daddy with his car and pipe

Grandma Callie and Grandpa Frank

CHAPTER 2

Becoming a Josephite

"Here I Am Lord"

THE HAPPIEST DAYS of my life were spent at Epiphany Apostolic College, situated in the picturesque Hudson Valley. For the first time, I experienced a northern winter in all of its beauty--the fluffy white snow covering the landscape, the glistening ice cycles on tree limbs, the slippery roads and the frozen ponds. This little southern boy enjoyed all of the fun that the ice and snow had to offer: ice skating, rides on the toboggan and snow ball fights.

Because I didn't have money to return home for Christmas and Easter, two of the older seminarians took me with them to spend the holidays with their families. Bill McKenna invited me to spend Christmas with the McKenna family in Boston. When I arrived, Mrs. McKenna let me know that I was also her "son" and that I was to attend morning Mass in the snow and help Bill with his chores. Believe me, she meant what she said! Thank goodness, my Mother had taught me to clean and perform other household chores. Mrs. McKenna fed us well and provided me with a memorable and happy Christmas. Bill and I became close friends. He served as my associate pastor at St. Brigid's in Los Angeles. He is now with his precious Mom in heaven. The family gave me his pyx (small round receptacle used to carry consecrated hosts) in his memory.

William Alerding brought me home with him to Boston to spend the Easter holidays with his family. Although it was difficult being away from home during this sacred and special church holy season, being with the Alerding family brought me much joy and peace. I thank God for their hospitality, love and encouragement.

After I finished high school I entered Epiphany College. My studies there were extremely difficult. My Mississippi education had not prepared me to compete with other seminarians, most of whom had been educated in the New York and Massachusetts educational systems. Fortunately, several other priests came to my rescue by giving me remedial classes and, Fr. Joseph Verrett, a black priest from New Orleans, took me under his wings and helped me with math and Latin. I soon caught up and began to maintain good grades.

There were three other southern young men in my immediate class— All African Americans: Vernon Moore, St. Peter Claver Parish, Mobile, AL; Thomas Honore', St. Francis Xavier Parish, Baton Rouge, LA; and Michael Nicholas, Notre Dame Parish, St. Martinsville, LA. We bonded together as a class; enjoying each other's companionship and sharing our gifts in support of one another. In addition to the winter sports, we enjoyed hand ball, basketball, and occasionally putting on plays.

All of us missed being with our families during the Christmas and Easter holidays so, one Christmas we saved our money and rented a car to drive home. What a happy decision that was! While travelling through North Carolina, one of our front tires blew out at nine-thirty in the evening. Needless to say, we were frightened: four Black boys stranded on a North Carolina road at night in the late 1950's. While still gripped by alarm and fear, we noticed a house with lights still on. We decided to send Tom Honore', a Creole with a light complex-ion, to go to the house and seek help. He nervously knocked on the door but was tempted to return to the car when he noticed that the woman had come to the door in her nightgown. After listening to our story, she called AAA for us. What a relief, God is good!

I was not a good math student. My math professor used the Bell Curve to grade and I was placed at the bottom of the curve. He informed me that I was the least likely in my class to survive. He tried to have me dismissed from the seminary by failing me in math. That dark cloud of rejection had again extended its ugly shadow over my dreams. I was rescued by my Spiritual Director, Fr. Peter Hogan. When I pointed out to Fr. Hogan that the professor had left the math exams on the radiator in the hallway after the test and had not even graded them, he confronted the professor and warned him that he had one more time to give me an unfair or failing grade. From then on, the professor reviewed all my math papers fairly and I ended the course with a "B" average. With a good grasp of math and Latin and the support of mentors, my anxiety began to ease a bit.

In 1958, I entered the novitiate in Walden, New York. The novitiate, a cloistered year of intense prayer, work, and study, was a true blessing for me. I loved becoming immersed in Josephite spirituality. Community prayer became an especially meaningful and important part of my day.

My Novice Director, Father Robert O'Connell, was a former pastor in my home parish. Father O'Connell was by no means a push over: he said what he meant and meant what he said. God help you if he had to remind you of anything a second time. He assigned me to be the driver for the novitiate. I have always loved to drive and I quickly learned how to drive in the snow. Being the driver, released me from other household chores and allowed me the unique privilege of getting out of the seminary and into the City of Newburg. As a result, I got to know a number of people in the city who were very supportive of me during my spiritual journey. Sister Mary Rose, who worked at the seminary, was a very special angel during my Novitiate. I could always be assured of her prayers and encouragement.

On completion of my year of novitiate, I was permitted to continue my studies at St. Joseph Seminary in Washington, DC. Though difficult (all of the theology classes were in Latin!), my life at St. Joseph Seminary in Washington, D.C. was a time of rich blessings for me. It was there that I grew fully into manhood and was filled with longing for pastoral ministry.

At the end of each academic year, several seminarians were sent to staff Camp Dineen in Poughkeepsie to work with troubled boys from New York City. Other seminarians were sent to summer school to prepare for teaching at one of our seminaries or at St. Augustine High School in New Orleans, a prestigious high school for Black boys established by the Josephites in 1951. I was sent to study at St. Michael College in Winooski, Vermont and, later on, to St. Bonaventure, in Olean, New York. Catholic University, within walking distance of our seminary, would not accept Black students. On June 4, 1964, I made my fourth promise of obedience to the Josephites and became a clerical deacon. What a happy day! The end of my seminary days was in sight! Later that year, I finally graduated with a Master's Degree in Philosophy and Education. Praise the Lord!

CHAPTER 3

"Thou Art a Priest Forever..."

"I'm Available to You"

SEVERAL MONTHS BEFORE my ordination, I received my chalice, a beautiful silver-plated cup with an onyx accent piece. I was so excited! My chalice was a gift from Velma Renfroe, my Aunt Delphine's adopted daughter. My excitement grew with each passing day leading up to ordination. Invitations were sent and people were responding to attend the ordination, First Mass and banquet. My parents were busy preparing for all of the festivities. They were also preparing for Paulette's high school graduation in San Antonio two months after my ordination. The stress caused my Mother's blood pressure to rise but she made it through and was filled with pride.

I was called to ordination on March 27, 1965, at St. Louis Basilica, in New Orleans, Louisiana. Because all four of us were from the South, we were given permission to be ordained outside of Washington, D.C. so that our families and friends could attend. What a glorious day it was despite the fact that my parents were late for the ceremony. As they traveled to New Orleans on a chartered bus with parishioners of St. Peter, family and friends, they were stopped by the Mississippi Highway Patrol who thought they were "Freedom Riders". They were only released when Fr. Lawlor noticed the bus on the side of the road and stopped to reassure the police that these were his parishioners. When I saw my parents enter the Basilica, my tears quickly evaporated and I was filled with joy.

The ordination, which was officiated by Archbishop John P. Cody, included much fanfare and glorious church music. At communion time, we were invited to give communion to our family members first. I was shocked out of my shoes when my father, a lifelong Methodist, came up for Communion. I said "Dad you can't receive Communion". He said: "Yes, Father, I am now a Catholic". I couldn't control my tears of joy and welcome.

I could not wait to begin my journey in the Josephite apostolate. My heart echoed the words of the gospel song: "I'm Available to You"

You gave me my hands, to reach out to man
To show him Your love and Your perfect plan
You gave me my ears, I can hear your voice so clear. I can hear
the cries of sinners, but can I wipe away their tears.

You gave me my voice, to speak Your words
To sing all Your praises, to those who never heard. But with my eyes I see a need for
more availability. I see hearts that have been broken, so many people to be free.
Lord, I'm available to you, my will I give to you
I'll do what you say do, use me Lord.
To show someone the way and enable me to say. My
storage is empty and I am available to you.

There were five of us ordained to the priesthood in the Society of St. Joseph of the Sacred Heart. vWhen my three classmates and I were ordained, the number of African American priests in the Society of St. Joseph more than doubled. Up to that point, there were only three Black Josephite priests. Because he was too ill to be ordained with his class the year before, Arthur Paquette, a Caucasian from Boston, was also ordained with us. Fathers Moore, Nicholas and Paquette are now deceased. Father Honore' is happily married and lives in Culver City, CA. I am the sole remaining member of the class in priestly ministry. God's providential plan for my life defied the odds, once again.

After the ordination, my family sat around talking as I opened the cards and gifts that I had received. We were all stunned when our Mother casually told us an incredible story. She was the only child of a single mother and was often left alone and lonely in a Chicago apartment while her mother went to work. During the summers, she visited her Godmother in Pascagoula where she enjoyed the companionship of other girls her age. Although she loved her mother, during one of those visits my mother made a girlish promise to give God her first born if He would allow her to stay in Pascagoula. God took her up on the promise by giving her first born child and only son a vocation to the priesthood. I feel very blessed to be a central part of such a special covenant between my mother and God.

My First Mass took place the next day at St. Peter the Apostle Church in Pascagoula on a beautiful Spring-like Sunday morning. It was a wonderful event. The church was overflowing with friends, family, and parishioners. My vestments and those of all of the concelebrants were made of gold lame'. I could hardly contain my emotions! That day marked the fulfillment of my life's dream. After a long and challenging journey, I was finally embarking on a lifetime of priestly ministry in the Catholic Church and the African American community. What a joy it was to consecrate the bread and wine for the first time, use my chalice and give Communion to my parents, sisters and friends!

My First Mass was followed by a delicious banquet in the school gymnasium. I sat at the head table with my parents, Grandma Kirt, Aunt Delphine, my siblings, and the pastor, Fr. Raphael Maggiore. There were at least two hundred people there; aunts, uncles, neighbors, childhood friends, cousins, classmates, and Josephite priests. It is a day that I will always remember.

On June 20, 1965, shortly after ordination, I was temporarily assigned to assist Father William ("Bill") Morrissey, S.S.J, in Natchez, MS. Father Morrissey welcomed me warmly to the Josephites' first and oldest parish in the Diocese of Jackson. (How ironic it was that, even though temporary, my first assignment was in the Diocese of Jackson where I was rejected as a candidate for the seminary.) Holy Family had two missions attached to it: St. John the Baptist Church in Cranfield and St. Ann's in Fayette.

Seminary Days and Ordination

Kitchen duty at the seminary

With Sister Rose and Grandma Kirt at Epiphany

Making final Promises

Ordination to the Diaconate
Shrine of the Immaculate Conception, Washington, D.C.

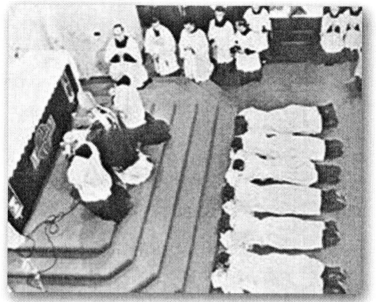

Ordination, St. Louis Cathedral in New Orleans

My ordination photo

My First Mass
St. Peter the Apostle, Pascagoula

Father Morrissey, the beloved pastor of Holy Family, enjoyed the respect of most of the citizens of Natchez. Ninety-nine percent of his time was spent fighting for the voting and other civil rights for Black citizens. He welcomed, housed and fed the Freedom Riders who came south to work in the Civil Rights Movement because white restaurants and hotels would not accommodate them.

Father Morrissey had worked closely with his friend and civil rights leader, Medgar Evers, before he was assassinated and still continued to do what he could two years later. Because he was usually away all day, he left the parish operations in my hands. Monsignor Thomas Fullum, who worked at the Cathedral, validated this responsibility by informing me that I was the "*de facto*" pastor. He told me to call him if I had difficulty making any decision. I was very grateful for the administrative skills that Father Lawlor had taught me. I used them extensively during my tenure at Holy Family.

At that time, Holy Family had both an elementary and a high school. I taught religion at the high school several days a week. This gave me the opportunity to get to know many of the students and get involved in their activities. One hot Sunday afternoon, the teens asked me if they could have a dance on the enclosed playground of the elementary school. To their delight and that of their parents, I consented.

An hour and a half after the dance began, the Natchez police knocked on the door. When I opened it, I was shocked by their apparent anger. They demanded that I send the teen band members out and told me that the dance was in violation of the "blue laws" of the State of Mississippi. I asked what specific "blue law" we had violated. He informed me that the "blue laws" prohibited dances on Sundays. One of the adult chaperones then told me that the police had plans to destroy the band members' instruments because when they played for a white teen group the night before, the white girls made advances toward the boys or vice-versa. In any case, the police wanted to harm the band members. I informed the police that they could not come onto the church grounds without a warrant. I then told the band members to take their instruments to the church sanctuary and I told the teens to call their parents to come pick them up. The Chief of Police, a fervent Catholic, was livid! He got on his car radio communication system and informed the police officers around the city and the Ku Klux Klan (KKK) that this tall Negro priest had refused to allow him to enter church property. He told me that I was a disgrace to the Catholic Church and that I needed to be more like his daughter who was a "holy nun".

I later learned that, after that incident, my name had been placed on the KKK's "not welcomed" list. I did not know that from the time of that incident until I left, the Klan followed me where ever I went--looking for an opportunity to "teach me a lesson". The Black cab drivers were tuned into the police radio transmission system so they were aware of the Klan's malicious intent. Whenever the police tailed me, one of the cab drivers also followed me. They were sorely aware that only a year earlier, James Chaney, Michael Schwerner, and Andrew Goodman had been murdered by the Klan members and their bodies buried off a dirt road in Meridian. The tension around the KKK and me continued for several months until the cab drivers finally informed my Superior of what was happening. Father Matthew O'Rourke called and told me that I was being followed. He immediately transferred me to fill-in at Our Mother of Mercy Parish in Fort Worth, Texas and St. Anthony Parish in Dallas where I remained until the end of the summer. It was good that Father O'Rourke moved me because I'm sure I would not have changed my behavior even if I had been aware of what was happening. I thank God for his protective vigilance over my life and wellbeing.

In 2014, during my tenure as Superior General of the Josephites, I had the privilege of attending the rededication of Holy Family Church in Natchez. The church had been in desperate need of major repairs: roof, drains, and a total refurbishing of the interior. Such repairs were beyond the financial capabilities of the aging parishioners. The Archives and History Department of the State of Mississippi offered to give the parish a grant to replace the roof if the parishioners could raise 20% of the proposed $169,000 grant. The parishioners worked tirelessly to raise the funds and, by the end of the fundraising campaign, they had surpassed the required amount. The badly deteriorated roof was removed from the two-story structure and replaced with a new one. During the re-roofing of the church, the State gave the parish a second grant of $80,000 to repaint the interior, refinish the pews, beautify the sanctuary and re-carpet the entire church. All of the money was contributed in memory and appreciation of Fr. Morrissey's courageous and outstanding work to advance the civil rights of Negro citizens in race-torn Natchez, Mississippi during the turbulent sixties.

The Church was filled to capacity for the rededication ceremony in 2014. Guests included the governor, the mayor, parishioners and countless members of city government--African American and Caucasian. A number of the parishioners still remembered my brief tenure at Holy Family and that notorious brush with the law. It was a memorable occasion and a tremendous tribute to the faith, commitment, fortitude and love of Father Bill Morrissey. His very close friend and working companion, Medgar Evers, had been assassinated in 1963, two years before I arrived. Though remnants of racial discrimination remain in Natchez (as they do everywhere), the fruits of the work of these two extraordinary men were clearly apparent in the assembly during the dedication of the newly renovated Holy Family Church.

CHAPTER 4

❦

"Each One, Teach One"

"Leaning on the Everlasting Arm"

MY FIRST PERMANENT assignment at St. Augustine High School (St. Aug) in New Orleans began on September 9, 1965. Founded by the Josephites in 1951, it was and remains the premier high school for African-American males in the country. At the time it was established, no other Catholic high school in New Orleans would accept Blacks.

My assignment included teaching remedial reading to some of the students on the C and D Tracts, serving as homeroom teacher for the B Tract students and teaching religion. I also chaired the Liturgy Department. For a first-year high school teacher, I had my hands full. I also had the privilege of establishing a Black Studies program for the students while at St. Aug.

In 1965, the St. Augustine Purple Knights were denied admission into the Louisiana High School Athletic Association (LHSAA) for the third time despite its acknowledged academic excellence and proven athletic prowess. Spearheaded by Father Joseph Verrett and with the full backing of the Josephites, the school and parents filed suit against the LHSAA based on its "systematic exclusion of Negro schools". The legal challenge was ultimately successful and resulted in the desegregation of high school athletics in the state of Louisiana. During the same time, the St. Aug Marching Purple Knights became the first "Negro" band to play in an all-white *Mardi Gras* parade in New Orleans. The school was breaking historic barriers in every arena.

During my first year of teaching at St. Aug, Daddy gave me a 1955 Plymouth that he had retrieved from the auto junk yard. He painted it a beautiful blue and immaculately reconditioned the interior. For many years, I proudly drove my Plymouth back and forth from St. Augustine to my home in Pascagoula, stopping each way in Oceans Springs to visit my favorite aunt, Henrietta Williams. Eating ice cream with her before leaving was a treasured ritual.

Having been away at the seminary for so many years, I relished the opportunity to go home frequently. It was always good to see my parents and eat some of Mom's good cooking. I love the outdoors so, as a young priest, I began saying my Office (official daily prayers of the Church) while walking back and forth between the pecan trees in our front yard. My dog often paced with me. The shaded and flower-lined yard was such a very peaceful setting for prayer and meditation. Neighborhood children would often greet me with: "Hey, Father 'Little Willie'". I continued this practice of pacing for most of my life. These days, I sit in a chair on the front porch to say my Office.

In August of 1969, the winds of Hurricane Camille hit the Gulf Coast and New Orleans with a savage blow. The Seventh and Ninth Wards suffered severe water and wind damage. St. Augustine High School offered shelter to hundreds of citizens living in the vicinity of the school. A massive clean-up of the Seventh Ward and St. Aug began immediately after the hurricane. It was a very challenging time for our students and their families and the Josepites helped in any way possible. Classes finally resumed in late September.

The five years that I spent at St. Augustine were some of the happiest years of my life! There were ten Josephites on the faculty and residing in the Josephite Faculty House. It reflected religious community life as it was meant to be and as it is seldom realized in parishes. We ate together, prayed together, laughed together, worked together and played together. We had rigorous and candid discussions on everything from politics to art and literature. We enjoyed each other's company and the privilege that was ours to provide a well-rounded education to the young and talented African American male students who attended the school.

For the last two years of my assignment at St. Aug, I was given the additional duties of serving as Assistant Spiritual Director and Director of Apostolic Activities for our Josephite Brothers who resided off campus at St. Joseph the Worker Training Center on St. Bernard Avenue. Father Edward Casserly, our Superior General, was set on pulling me into the Josephite Formation Program.

CHAPTER 5

Young, Gifted, Black and Catholic

"Great is Thy Faithfulness"

THESE WERE VERY exciting times in the Catholic Church and in the nation. The church was in the process of working to fully implement the mandates of Vatican II to be more culturally inclusive and engage the laity in every aspect of the liturgy and church administration. For the first time, people heard the Mass in their native languages and, because the altar was turned around, they could see everything that was going on. The mystery was no longer encrypted. Church music also changed to include other genres (i.e., folk music and Negro spirituals), instruments other than the organ, and new, more populist melodies and lyrics.

The nation was also working to implement its new and expanded civil rights laws to ensure the rights of all people to quality education, equal access to public accommodations, and fair and equal employment.

In August of 1968, at the height of the Civil Rights Movement, the National Black Catholic Clergy Caucus and the National Black Sisters' Conference convened their first joint meeting in Detroit, MI. It was not only a time of great transition in our nation, but also, post-Vatican II, it was a time of tremendous transition in the Catholic Church. It was in this potent atmosphere, rich with possibilities, that a great number of Black priests and sisters from almost all dioceses, religious Orders and Congregations in the United States, organized and committed themselves to build community, promote and develop Black leadership, and create culturally rich Africentric liturgical experiences in the Catholic Church. We worked together enthusiastically to affirm our identity and place in the church and to plan, encourage and implement the inclusion of African American cultural elements (including music, textiles, instruments, dance and emotional affirmations) into the Catholic liturgy. In the words of Nina Simone, we were "young, gifted, and black" and ready to take our places in the Church. It all resonated in my soul! Just three years before, the first African American bishop in modern times, Bishop Harold Perry, was ordained in the American Catholic Church.* We were very proud to be in religious life and empowered and anxious to share our talents with the Church and the people of God, especially Black Catholics, most of whom had never seen a black priest or sister!

I am acknowledged as a founding member of the National Black Clergy Caucus and the National Black Sisters Conference. I was also elected Co-Chairman of the newly established National Office of Black Catholics' (NOBC) Seminary Program. While serving in that position, I was asked to write an article, "The Meaning of Black Liturgy", for Freeing the Spirit magazine, a publication of the Black Liturgy Committee of the NOBC. I felt that it was especially important for the Josephites, whose mission it is to serve African American Catholics, to be on the front lines of enculturating the liturgy. I felt personally compelled to do all that I could to help make this happen.

In addition to the NOBC, other church-affiliated institutions and organizations such as the Institute for Black Catholic Studies at Xavier University of Louisiana and the National Black Catholic Congress (an umbrella organization) sprung up and provided invaluable opportunities for African American Catholics to learn more about our value and contributions to the Church throughout the ages. We realized anew that our culture exemplifies a strong faith in a loving

---

* Father James Healy was the first Catholic bishop of African descent however he presented himself and identified more with his Irish ancestry.

God; family and community; a shared experience of trials and deliverance; joy in the saving grace of Jesus, our brother; compassion and empathy for the poor and downtrodden; a holistic response to life and faith—body, soul, emotions and intellect. These are the values that I learned in my family as a child. It filled me with joy to know that I could reinforce and exemplify them in the liturgy of the Church that I loved and now served. It is all captured in our music: particularly, gospel music.

Empowered by the mandates of Vatican II and a spirit of unity, most of the Black Catholic clergy left the first National Black Clergy Caucus Conference eager to affirm and share expressions of our cultural values with our African American Catholic brothers and sisters around the country. We understood clearly that affirmation of our culture did not mean negating the blended and diverse cultural practices expressed in the Roman Catholic liturgy as we knew it. We also understood that, as family members moved from their small communities to large cities seeking educational and employment opportunities, the affirmation of our culture was critical to sustaining it.

In September of 1970, I was reassigned to teach Black Studies and serve as Spiritual Director of the seminarians at our St. Joseph Seminary in the District of Columbia. Before beginning my new assignment at the seminary, I asked the Superior, Father Mathew O'Rourke, for permission to study in Africa. I felt that this would give me the grounding in the African culture that I needed (and for which I yearned) to continue my pursuit of African American Studies. Permission was granted and I registered for the teacher exchange program at Howard University. Twenty-five African American teachers journeyed from Washington to West Africa (Togo, Nigeria, Ghana and Sierra Leone). After a summer of studying at the universities in these countries, I returned to St. Joseph seminary prepared to teach our seminarians. However, this was not to be. As soon as I returned, the Superior made me Chairman of the Josephite Liturgy Committee and informed me that he wanted me to consider being a pastor in Washington, D.C. My facial expression left no doubt that I was utterly confused. He told me "the Josephites have an opportunity to assign a second black pastor on the East Coast". After catching my breath, I asked: "May I bring black spirituality and culture into the parish liturgy and develop strong Black Catholic leadership?" His Irish smile enveloped me. "That is why I chose you. Your associate pastor will be Father Jim Didas, your former rector. He will understand what you want to do and will support your work." And, that he did. The Didas-Norvel partnering was a marriage made in heaven!

Father Didas was a brilliant man who had the opportunity to study English under the renowned, Bishop Fulton J. Sheen. He did not complete the course however, because Bishop Sheen recognized that Fr. Didas knew more English than he. Fr. Didas was invited to leave Bishop Sheen's class with his degree and without having completed the course.

CHAPTER 6

"Order My Steps"

I BEGAN MY pastorate at St. Benedict the Moor Parish on September 15, 1971 becoming the second African American Catholic priest appointed as a pastor in Washington, D.C. Of course, I wanted to begin immediately infusing Black culture into the liturgy however, I wanted to make sure that I would not ruffle too many feathers so, I went to Archbishop Patrick O'Boyle to inform him of what I was planning to do. I was aware that several priests in the archdiocese had recently been suspended for tampering with the liturgy. I presented a letter to the Archbishop explaining that, what I wanted to do, would involve using a piano and a Protestant choir director in the Sunday liturgy. He read the letter and immediately put it back into the envelope and handed it back to me. "Do", he said, "and don't write to me again about this request." I was encouraged and inspired by his consent.

One of the primary issues that confronted me when I arrived at St. Benedict was the absence of any financial records for employees. The parish was incurring exorbitant fines from the IRS related to unpaid employee taxes for the school and church. I looked everywhere and asked several people where the files were (including the previous pastor), but still came up empty. Everyone told me that the records were in the file cabinet but they were nowhere to be found. As a rookie pastor with no financial background, I was totally frustrated. I decided to call on one of the permanent deacons, Mr. Paul Perneky, whom I had taught at the seminary, to assist me. He was a CPA and I was sure that he could help. After learning that there were no files available, Paul contacted the IRS and arranged to pay the fees and fines. He then established a financial system for the parish including ledgers to record all transactions. He trained me on what to do and how to do it. He worked to ensure that I never found myself in that position again. And, I didn't. One of the first things that I did in each parish that I went to from that point forward was to balance the books and hire an accountant.

After I got a handle on the financial situation, I immediately began to infuse the liturgy with our spirituality and culture. I was practically stopped dead in my tracks however, by the reactions of the parishioners. They had great difficulty getting onboard with my enculturation plan and affirming their black identity in the liturgy. They were Roman Catholic to the core and did not want all that "Baptist worship" in their church. They did not realize that the Roman Catholic Mass ritual as we knew it was developed over time by including European cultural practices. They did not realize that African Americans had not only been encouraged by Vatican II to contribute our cultural gifts to the church in the liturgy, but also mandated to do so. They did not understand that our cultural gifts are enriching and life-giving—not just to us but to anyone who is open to receive and appreciate them. They did not understand that the gifts of our Black spirituality and culture are indeed very special gifts from God. And, finally, they did not understand or appreciate that African American Baptists had, fortunately, preserved much of our spirituality and culture in their worship services.

The resistance and fear of my parishioners let me know that I needed to slow down and set-up workshops to help them understand and to reassure them that including our culture in the liturgy would enhance, not adulterate it. I had to assure them that the Roman spirituality and liturgy in which they were presently immersed, was still valid and good and would never be eliminated. What I was trying to establish was not a matter of either/or but a matter of both/and. I could see clearly that this would be a process.

In the early 1970's when my pastorate began at St. Benedict the Moor, Washington, D.C. was still vulnerable to the effects of race riots. The city was unsettled and its citizens were fearful of "those unruly blacks" who could still reek destruction on their homes and communities. I was a bit disturbed when

I found out sometime later that several of my brother priests had added to that fear by telling my parishioners not to "allow Bill Norvel to bring that black stuff" into their church. This interference and lack of vision only served to strengthen the resistance that I encountered.

I began changing the church environment by hanging two beautiful banners on either wall of our assembly. One stated: "God in His Goodness has made me black and beautiful"; the other stated: "black is not a color, but an experience". I removed the main crucifix hanging above the tabernacle and replaced it with a beautiful ebony corpus of the suffering Jesus attached to a cross. My sister, Kirt, had made a beautiful Africentric vestment for me which I wore for Mass. When the Monday evening worshippers came for Mass and Novena, they stood in utter disbelief as they stared at those unwelcomed additions to their worship space. They didn't say a word to me but, when they got home, they got on the phone. Within an hour, eighty-five percent of my parishioners had learned about the banners and the corpus. Mrs. Zelks had not been able to see the banners that night because of her poor eyesight. She returned to the church the next morning and said: "Son, let me see those banners and the crucifix they are talking about." When I showed them to her, she said: "Father, don't take them down".

As time went on, the objections increased and the anger was more intense. It was a very stressful time for me and it began to show in my demeanor. Mr. and Mrs. Mahoney noticed and called to invite me to come to their home for tea! I was surprised and amused by their invitation to tea (rather than coffee), nevertheless, I went to their home. As we were sipping our tea, they told me that they did not want me to break under the stress I was enduring. "We are now seventy-five years of age," she said. "We have longed to have our black identity celebrated in our church. You are the priest who is making this happen. You must not stop now." I left with their blessing and assurance of support.

This experience with the Mahoneys gave me the courage to initiate workshops to educate my parishioners on Black spirituality and give them the opportunity to express their objections openly. At this point, I was blessed not to take their objections personally. I understood where they were emotionally and that they had only a limited understanding of what I was trying to do and why. I assured them that God made our blackness and that He declared all that He made to be "good". "If that is so, and surely it is, we are not in a position to say that He is wrong," I told them. I also informed them that the Holy Father, Paul VI, told us that we are now of age and that it is time to share our blackness and culture with the Catholic Church. "Our Black cultural values, experiences, and spirituality are our gift to the Catholic Church," I said.

Our culture and spirituality are expressed in the liturgy not only in Negro spirituals and gospel music but also in religious vestments, art, peaching, scriptural proclamations, sacred movement, and prayer styles. The sacred beats and rhythms resonate with us and inspire us to worship God with our entire bodies, making a "joyful noise to the Lord"—with clapping, dancing, and resounding acclamations of "Amen". In this way, God is praised authentically and whole-heartedly by His people in His holy place.

I hired Avon Gillespie, a renowned Gospel musician and dance teacher to teach sacred movement; Rev. Ezekiel Thomas, who became our gospel choir director; and, Rev. Robert Pipes, who helped me develop a Black leadership initiative. Later when I needed to replace Rev. Thomas, I hired Rawn Harbor as Choir Director. What a blessing that choice turned out to be! At the time, Rawn was Baptist. He is now the top black Catholic musician and liturgist in the country. Last, but not least, I taught liturgy. I established a gospel choir with twelve people who didn't think I was crazy. Over a period of a year and a half, our gospel choir grew to thirty-five members. The liturgy and the choir developed so well that Black Catholics were attracted from parishes throughout Washington, suburban Maryland and Virginia to join in the celebration of our liturgy. If you weren't seated by 10:00 a.m. on Sunday, you would not be able to find a seat at St. Benedict's 10:30 Mass. A number of Protestants in the community also chose to worship with us.

Respecting the spirituality of all my parishioners, I celebrated two Masses on Sunday: the Gospel Mass at 10:30 a.m. and the 7:30 a.m. traditional Mass in which "the four squares" (traditional entrance, offertory, communion and recessional hymns) were sung. However, I always had the music director play a Negro spiritual for the Post Communion hymn. I knew that this would touch them emotionally and gently help them to get back in touch with the beautiful spirituality they had suppressed for many years. This gentle exposure to Negro spirituals gradually softened the hearts of those who attended the 7:30 Mass. Eventually, many of them switched to the 10:30 gospel Mass.

Once the parishioners became comfortable with the new liturgy, I began to have "Altar Call". After the sermon, I invited everyone to the foot of the altar who felt that they had a special need for physical, emotional, psychological or spiritual healing. The congregation stretched their hands over the group and I called on the Holy Spirit to shower His healing blessings on each individual and their families. The parishioners were a bit reluctant at first but this soon became a treasured part of the liturgy. Those who were in need, experienced and appreciated the power and assurance of community prayer on their behalf and those who did not come to the altar, were grateful for the opportunity to support their brothers and sisters with prayer. We often tell one another that we will pray for them and fail to do so, or, we are not aware of the trials of our friends and are therefore, not able to support them in their time of need. This ritual allowed us to pray for one another in a special way without having to know the specifics of their concerns. I continued this ritual at every parish that I served as pastor.

In the mid-1970's, I took the gospel choir on a concert tour to Josephite parishes in the south to show them how gospel music should be used in our liturgies. We were received well by some parishes but not by others. My home parish of St. Peter the Apostle initiated a gospel choir soon after we left. It is still going strong. When it began, my Mother and Father joined and were known as the "mom and pop" of the gospel choir. My Mother had never sung in a choir but she signed up and signed my Dad up also. She told him: "You sing spirituals all the time in the yard, you can sing them in the choir." Daddy was also elected Chaplain of the choir.

It was very important to me and, I felt very necessary, to establish strong and informed Black leadership in the church. My parishioners were invited to take ownership of their church. With the help of Rev. Robert Pipes, I established an informed Parish Council that took the well-being of the church to the parishioners, sought their input, and welcomed the contributions of their talents, skills and finances. The Youth Committee reached out in ministry to all of our adolescents, teens and young adults. The St. Vincent de Paul Society fed the hungry and helped the needy in our neighborhood. Our Prison Ministry reached out to our brothers and sisters in the D.C. jail and at Lorton Prison. In a short period of time, the parish was bustling with life, activity and community service. Membership grew to over 900 people.

Word of our gospel liturgy began to spread far and wide. The U. S. Conference of Catholic Bishops heard about what I was doing and asked me to cooperate with Maryknoll magazine to describe and document the gospel liturgy. The article was published in the magazine in May of 1974. During the summer of 1973, I was invited to teach a summer program, "Ministering in the African American Community", at the University of Notre Dame. Professors at Catholic University School of Liturgy heard about our Gospel Mass and assigned students in the department to attend Mass, observe what was being done to implement the mandated liturgical changes, and write a critique. The only negative comment they reported in the critique was that I was not using the newly revised Lectionary for Mass. They decided to purchase a new Lectionary as a gift to the parish. Many of the students continued to worship with us on Sundays. These experiences, among others, were confirmation that what I was doing was right and good.

The vibrant life of the parish was also reflected on the campus of our elementary school. The Oblate Sisters of Providence taught in the school and were wonderful role models for our students. Sr. Clementina Givens was principal when I first arrived and Sr. Charlotte Marshall was principal when Sr. Clementina was transferred. Both of them ran tight ships and ensured that students met or exceeded academic standards. I worked well with both of them and under their leadership, our students prospered. The children wore their uniforms with great pride! They were proud to be black, Catholic and students of St. Benedict the Moor School.

While at St. Benedict the Moor, I was called by a woman from one of our parishes in the south to come to the aid of one of my best friends who was pastor at the church she attended. He was apparently having a mental breakdown and had locked himself in the rectory refusing to respond to anyone. He would not even respond to our Superior, Father Matthew O'Rourke. The parishioner called me with the hope that the priest would respond to me.

I immediately boarded a plane and went directly to the parish rectory. I rang the doorbell many times and called out to announce myself. Father finally responded and invited me into the rectory. After a lengthy discussion, I convinced him to return with me to St. Benedict the Moor where I would seek medical help for him. He agreed to come with me. When we returned to Washington, I called the Superior and told him that my friend was with me and that another priest should be sent to take his place. Father O'Rourke thanked me and asked me to keep him with me as long as I thought he needed to be there.

One Sunday after the celebration of the Masses, I had the job of counting the collection. Soon after I finished counting, had bagged the approximately $8,000 and prepared it for deposit, the doorbell rang. I ran down the stairs to answer it. The man at the door told me that he was experiencing car trouble and asked if he could use the phone to call for help. I let him in to make the call. After entering the rectory, he pulled out a gun and demanded our money. In anticipation of just such a possibility, parishioners had stuffed several bags with fake money for my use. Unfortunately, the robber opened the bag before leaving and became outraged at my attempt to con him. He immediately began searching for the real money. He bound me and my brother priest from the south (who was still with me receiving medical help) with duck-tape and moved us to the boiler room. The robber was still so angry that he pulled the washing machine connection from the wall and water began flowing everywhere. He ordered us to lay down on the floor in the water. The other priest, who didn't care whether he lived or died, refused to lie down in the water. I hit him forcefully on the back of his legs and he fell down on the floor. The robber then went upstairs to the second floor where he found the bagged money on a table. He returned to the boiler room, brought us upstairs, locked us in a closet and left. We waited a while and then I yelled for several hours until someone finally heard us and came to our rescue.

Fortunately, I was able to describe the robber to the police. He was familiar to many in the community so they were able to help the police find and apprehend him. I later identified the thief in a line up at the police station.

One of the major challenges and accomplishments of my tenure as pastor of St. Benedict the Moor was the construction of a $900,000 parish hall which we named the Imperial Room. At the time, we only had a small multi-purpose room to use for Mass. It was converted from a church to an event space by rotating the altar. There was no real place for fellowship or church activities and definitely not enough room to celebrate the gospel Mass.

Aware that the Archbishop had refused to allow his priests to borrow money from the bank, nevertheless, I went to Archbishop O'Boyle to request permission to build. To my surprise, he gave his consent. I was again encouraged by the confidence he showed in me as a young priest in my first parish assignment. When his priests questioned him later about why I had gotten permission to build and they had not, I was told he replied: "If Bill Norvel borrows money, he will pay it off. If I give you permission to borrow, I will end up having to pay off the debt."

Although several of the parishioners challenged the decision to build the Imperial Room, declaring, among other things, that there was not enough land, that did not stop me. The Imperial Room soon became a reality. It is a large hall the size of a basketball court, with bleachers on one side wall, a full stage on the other and a $20,000 kitchen. On Sundays, the space was used for the gospel Mass because the multi-purpose room was now too small for that Mass. On Friday evenings, the Imperial Room was used for bingo and, on school days, as the school cafeteria. On many Friday and Saturday evenings, it was rented out for cabarets or wedding receptions.

Because my parishioners did not frequent the Kennedy Center for entertainment, I decided to provide entertainment in the community. Over the years, I booked Sarah Vaughn, Earl "Fatha" Hines, Count Basie and other famous entertainers for cabarets in the Imperial Room. Ms. Queen, our parish chef, prepared delicious meals for the cabaret guests and a good time was had by all.

The Quander Room, which was on the front end of the Imperial Room, was named for one our parishioners, Mr. Edward Quander, who faithfully provided assistance around the church property. Weekly meetings of the Golden Age Club, a community group of seniors, were held there.

The day the Imperial Room was dedicated was a glorious day that I was able to share with my parents and sisters who came to be with me. You should have seen our Dad; he was the proudest man in the District of Columbia and he let everyone know it. One of my parishioners, who had criticized everything I did in the parish, took my Dad aside and apologized for his behavior toward me. He complimented me to my father for doing a good job. Dad was happy to share this information with me.

Of course, Mom exercised her culinary skills in the rectory kitchen by preparing a pot of Creole gumbo and baking a pound cake. This delighted Father Didas, my Associate Pastor. He would have had no objection if Mom had decided to stay at St. Benedict.

I ended my seven-year pastorate at St. Benedict the Moor in 1977. During those years, I made many wonderful life-long friends. I was also blessed to have had two outstanding pastoral assistants who whole-heartily supported my ministry there: Father James Didas and Father Thomas "Tom" Frank.

Father Didas, who was previously my rector for six years at St. Joseph Seminary, was initially assigned as my Associate. Older and wiser than me, he humbly addressed the fears and anxieties of our parishioners as I worked to introduce Black culture in the parish. If I proceeded more rapidly than our parishioners could accept, he would caution me to slow down to let them catch-up with me. He was indeed an "angel" in disguise.

Father Tom, whom I had in diaconal formation, became my Associate Pastor when Father Didas was transferred. He was also a blessing. He took pride in helping to develop the leadership initiative and liturgy in the parish. Together, we provided a holistic pastoral ministry to Black Catholics in northeast Washington, D.C.: education and activities for the youth, religious and leadership training for adults, visitation for the sick and shut-in, social justice and community outreach initiatives, meaningful fellowship, and, of course, the sacraments and a liturgy that was engaging, spiritually gratifying, and culturally authentic. To God be the glory!

My experience at St. Benedict the Moor was extremely enriching and fruitful.

I felt confident and encouraged about what could be done to include and empower my people in the Catholic Church. My heart was full of joy. It was very difficult to leave.

CHAPTER 7

$\cdotp$

Pioneering the West Coast

"He's Blessing Me"

IN 1977, THE Superior General, Father John Filippelli, called me to Headquarters in Baltimore to ask if I would consider taking an assignment in Los Angeles. At the urging of former Josephite parishioners who had moved to Los Angeles from the south, Cardinal James McIntyre asked the Josephites to come to Los Angeles to serve them. The Superior responded by sending me to become the first Josephite to pastor a church on the west coast. I was asked to choose among three churches that were being offered to us. I chose St. Brigid because it had more parishioners from former Josephite parishes. The pastor, Fr. Francis Seymore, welcomed me to the parish on November 14, 1977 as did Deacon Gil Lanoix and Sr. Marianna Halsmer, S.S.S., my new Pastoral Assistant.

St. Brigid is a large church which can comfortably seat thirteen hundred worshippers. It was the victim of white flight after the 1965 riots in Watts, the neighborhood adjacent to the church. The area had not fully recovered from the devastation of the riots. As a result of this and dynamics in the parish, St. Brigid's membership had declined dramatically. Three quarters of the pews had been roped off because of non-use and the front doors had not been used in twelve years! Parishioners only used the side entrance to enter and leave the sanctuary.

A handful of parishioners from New Orleans ruled the church with an iron fist. Parishioners with dark complexions were not welcomed. Leadership of all the organizations in the church was controlled by two families who made all of decisions for the parish. Parish Council meetings were held in one of their homes and the pastor was not invited! The semblance of a gospel Choir was shabby and not very conducive to liturgical worship. Needless to say, I had my hands full.

First of all, I had to make it clear that I was the pastor, that I made all decisions and that, from then on, Council meetings were to be convened on church property. The leaders strongly objected and told me that they would continue to hold Council meetings in their homes. To their dismay, I immediately disbanded the Parish Council and the choir, whose director also refused to respect my decisions.

During the next three weeks before establishing a new Parish Council and a new gospel choir (both were now open to all parishioners), Sister Marianna and I began visiting the homes of parishioners who had stopped attending St. Brigid and invited them to return. I assured them that all parish organizations would be under new leadership. After coming to Mass for a couple of months to make sure things would be changed, they renewed their membership.

We established a new Parish Council after several weeks of leadership training conducted by the very capable, Mrs. Marian Fussey. Membership on the Council was open to all parishioners except the former Parish Council members. I started a gospel choir with twelve brave parishioners and the help of Mr. Avon Gillespie who resided in Monterey, CA and Mrs. Margaret Dureaux, composer of "Give Me a Clean Heart"—both renown gospel music pioneers. Mrs. Dureaux served as our gospel choir director until I found a permanent director, Mr. Charles Johnson. I used the experience and knowledge that I had acquired at St. Benedict the Moor to organize the new choir, which soon grew by leaps and bounds. As it grew in size and reputation, hundreds of African American Catholics were drawn to St. Brigid for Sunday Mass. Within a year and a half, the front doors were re-opened and the roped used to isolate the front section of the church for 200 people on Sundays, was removed. Eventually, I had to purchase chairs to place in the aisles and in the choir loft to accommodate the increased number of worshippers. The total capacity of the church was 1,300. It was now overflowing on Sundays. Worshippers came from South Central Los Angeles and the St. Gabriel Valley. The choir was indeed, "the talk of the town".

One Sunday morning a disabled worshipper was making his way into the church with significant difficulty. I asked him if I could help. He said "No. You do the preaching and let the choir do the singing. That will make it all worthwhile."

St. Brigid Elementary School had been closed for several years before I arrived. We used the school for Religious Education with Mrs. Marian Fussey as its principal. She was also the parish secretary. The cultural enrichment program being taught at the church was also being infused into the religious education curriculum. The children learned about the significant contributions that African Americans have made throughout history to the church, science, mathematics, art, music, business, technology, education, and literature.

I was indeed blessed to have had Father Eli Bowens, S.S.J. as my able Pastoral Associate. Father Eli was a self-motivated young priest who involved himself totally in the ministry of developing an Africentric liturgical service and Black leadership. This ministry is what inspired him to become a Josephite. Being a part of the growth at St. Brigid was, for him, the fulfillment of a dream. Unfortunately, Father Eli passed away while at St. Brigid. He was mourned and sorely missed by the entire parish family.

Sister Marianna Halsmer, S.S.S. provided pastoral care for the sick of the parish and spearheaded outreach programs to the needy. With the ministerial support of Deacon Lanoix, pastoral services were caringly and efficiently provided to our growing parish.

After the confidence of the parishioners was restored and training was provided, I had no problem recruiting people for leadership roles. The parishioners readily and eagerly came forth to serve in the Youth Ministry, Altar Servers ministry, St. Vincent de Paul Society, Legion of Mary, AIDs Ministry, Prayer Ministry for the Home Bound and, as Extraordinary Ministers of the Eucharist. St. Brigid was taking every opportunity to bring the good news of salvation to our community.

Our Parish Council spread its tentacles into every area of the parish and assumed ownership of its growth and well-being. After a short period of time, we were able to pay off our debt to the Archdiocese and take full financial responsibility for the parish.

My family came to spend Christmas with me in 1982. After my sisters left, I took my parents to visit Methodist Bishop Charles Golden and his wife, Ida, who were family friends from Mississippi now living in Los Angeles.

Mrs. Golden had lived in Jackson, Mississippi where my mother was born and knew quite a bit about my mom's step-siblings. After we had been in their home for a while, she told my mother that her step-sister, Mable, lived only five blocks away. Bishop Golden had repeatedly advised his wife not to get involved but, knowing Mable and my mom, Ida felt it was the right thing to do. My mom was aware that she had a step-sister and brother but she had never met them. I encouraged Mrs. Golden to call Mable. She did, and Mable came right over. Mable showed up about a half hour later dressed almost identically to my mom! They immediately realized and acknowledged that they were sisters and warmly embraced one another. Two years later, Mable stood with my parents when they renewed their vows for their fiftieth wedding anniversary. Mable's other siblings, their spouses, and children also came from Jackson, MS to be with our family for the anniversary celebration. My mother, who had lived to age sixty-nine as an only child, now had a wonderful new family that was fully embraced by the Norvel clan.

We remain in contact with Aunt Mable by phone, cards, and visits, whenever possible. She is our only remaining aunt on either side of the family. On April 17, 2016, she celebrated her ninety-ninth birthday! She is beautiful, very loquacious, very interesting and entertaining. A former social worker, she is a remarkable woman, with a remarkable memory, and a heart full of love for people and God.

Four years into my pastorate, we gave thanks to God for the revitalization of St. Brigid Parish: our Eucharistic celebrations were spiritually nurturing, our gospel choir was making a name for itself in the Archdiocese, our Youth Ministry was addressing the needs of adolescents and teens and the parish leadership was not only spurring a growth in membership but also exemplifying their pride as Black Catholics. Through the good people at St. Brigid, God's blessings were touching me and the lives of countless souls in South Central Los Angeles.

In addition to my work at the church, I was engaged and working with the Ecumenical Fellowship (a group of inter-denominational pastors in the community) to help improve conditions for people in the community and served on the Board of the Southern Christian Leadership Conference. As a result of my work with these outstanding organizations, I was named Pastor of the Year in 1983 and received a Service Award from Loyola Marymont University.

Another good example of St. Brigid's outreach and con munity building was the experience we had with the local Black Muslims. We opened the church doors and welcomed them to have their religious service at our church when the foundation of their Mosque had been compromised by a minor earthquake. At the conclusion of our last Mass on Sunday, a crew of Muslims came to thoroughly clean our church in preparation for their afternoon worship service. I removed the Blessed Sacrament from the tabernacle and we were prepared to welcome our neighbors. They came, they worshipped and they expressed profound gratitude for our hospitality.

As an expression of their gratitude for our generosity and hospitality in their time of need, our Muslim friends came to the Farewell Banquet that was held for me at the Regency West and provided additional security. God continues to work in mysterious ways.

To my chagrin, the Lord called me to another ministry in 1983. I was elected Consultor General of the Society of St. Joseph on October 1st of that year which required that I transfer back to Baltimore. Moving to Baltimore from Los Angeles was one of the most painful separations I have ever experienced. My six years at St. Brigid had been some of the happiest and most productive of my ministry. I literally cried all the way to Las Vegas. I finally stopped, rested for a bit, dried my tears, broke the physical and emotional ties to St. Brigid, and then continued on to "Charm City".

CHAPTER 8

❦

"He's an On Time God"

As Consultor General, I was a member of the Executive Committee of the General Council of the Society of St. Joseph and was charged with representing the priests at Council meetings. I maintained contact with the priests to determine their needs and views with regard to the Society. Those four years were the least stimulating and engaging of my Josephite ministry. I did not feel that my gifts were being used to the fullest and I missed parish life. I felt totally disconnected from the community that I wished to serve.

The Lord came to my rescue with my election as the President of the National Black Catholic Clergy Caucus which was based at St. Augustine Parish in Washington, D.C. He is indeed, "an on time God!" I drove daily from Baltimore to Washington to assume my responsibilities as President of the Caucus.

From the beginning, my work was cut out for me--the Caucus was virtually bankrupt and the financial records were in disarray. With the help of my secretary, Ruby Robertson, I began the tasks of accounting for the grants that had been awarded to the Caucus from the U.S. Conference of Catholic Bishops, balancing the books, and collecting the past dues from our members. I acquired a $25,000 grant from the Josephites which I put into a savings account for future use. After a couple of years, the Caucus was back on its feet and effectively serving its members: Black priests, permanent deacons, Brothers, and seminarians.

In addition to the Black Clergy Caucus, I was a consultant to Black Catholic Parishes in the United States, a member of the Liturgical Commission in Baltimore, an advisor for the Josephite Harvest (the oldest Catholic periodical in the country), and served on the Black Liturgy Sub-Committee of the Bishops' Committee on Liturgy. Over the years, the Josephite Pastoral Center and archives have served as tremendous resources to me, my parishioners, Black Catholics, and clergy as we worked to build community, enrich the liturgy, and train Black Catholic church leaders. The Pastoral Center was established in 1966 to develop a Josephite Social Action Department to meet the needs of the poor in education, employment, housing and family life. It is still the "go to" place for religious education materials, pastoral programs, teacher-parent in-service training materials, creative resources for parishes, institutions and dioceses. The Josephite archives is the most comprehensive collection of information on Black Catholics in the country.

One of the most special honors that I had as President of the National Black Catholic Clergy Caucus was supporting and approving the publication of the first edition of "Lead Me, Guide Me" under the auspices of the Black Clergy Caucus. This initiative, spearheaded by Bishop James P. Lyke, was the first African American Catholic hymnal ever to be published. My endorsement as President of the Black Clergy Caucus is documented in the front of the hymnal.

My ministry at the Office of the National Black Catholic Clergy Caucus was a life-saver for me. It allowed me to use my skills, creativity and energy to the fullest. Most importantly, I got to know and work with some of the most extraordinary Black clergy in the country—priests, brothers, sisters, deacons and seminarians. It was an enriching and fulfilling experience. In 1985, I had the privilege of attending the Forty-Third International Eucharistic Congress in Nairobi, Kenya attended by Pope John Paul II. My Good Shepherd was still leading and guiding me in His service.

CHAPTER 9

On the Azalea Trail

"His Eye is on the Sparrow"

THE TERMINATION OF my assignment as Consultor General couldn't have come soon enough for me. At the end of my four-year term, I asked the Superior to assign me to a parish in the south so that I could help care for my parents whose health was beginning to fail. October 31, 1987, I was very pleased to be assigned pastor of Most Pure Heart of Mary Parish in Mobile, AL, only thirty-nine miles away from my parents. Sister Marianna and I were warmly received by the parishioners.

I still chuckle when I remember how the church leaders responded when I told them that I would be bringing with me a Sister of Social Service to serve as my pastoral associate. When they saw her picture, they responded: "What can this little old white lady do for us?" I told them to wait and see. Sister Marianna came and soon began using her wisdom and skills to care for the sick, make home visits and set up committees to serve the social needs of the parishioners. The parishioners quickly became attached to her.

Needless to say, I immediately began the process of introducing Black spirituality into the liturgy. That was a bad mistake. Sixteen years after I had established the first gospel choir in Washington, D.C., I had again made an erroneous assumption that my parishioners were ready to express their cultural identity in the Catholic liturgy.

The assumption was not entirely half-baked for, indeed, Black Catholics at Heart of Mary had a history of being progressive and asserting their cultural identity. In 1909, under the leadership of four Josephite priests, they established the fraternal order of the Knights of Peter Claver because they were not accepted into the Knight of Columbus. Again, in the early 1940s, with the leadership of another Josephite, Father Vincent Warren, parishioners became active in civil rights and supported the initiative to open a hospital for "colored people" (named Blessed Martin de Porres, a black saint) to assure the safe delivery of their babies and, eventually, quality general medical services for the "Colored" citizens of Mobile. And in 1962, Alexis Herman (former U.S. Secretary of Labor), a young Heart of Mary high school student, stole away from her school group to challenge Bishop Thomas J. Toolen about the treatment of Black students. When she slipped into the tent where the bishop was vesting, she asked him why Black Catholic students were never allowed to crown the Virgin Mary at the annual city-wide May Crowning Ceremony and why Black Catholic children were always last in the Christ the King Parade. Although she was suspended from school for doing this, Black Catholic students were eventually allowed to participate fully in the ceremony. And, finally, even though the liturgy in Black parishes around the country had become more culturally authentic over the past twenty years, the parishioners at Heart of Mary were not prepared to move forward by incorporating black cultural elements in their church and liturgy.

Many of the more vocal members of the parish took pride in being Creole so, they often found it difficult to embrace their Black culture. In spite of the resistance, I proceeded to develop plans to start a gospel choir. Mrs. Carolyn Smoke, a Methodist, was hired to be the choir director. Gradually, she established an enviable choir. I used my previous experience to weave gospel music into the liturgy. After about six months, most of the parishioners began to enjoy the gospel music worship experience and to be proud of their rich African American heritage.

Mrs. Smoke quickly and happily settled into her role as choir director at Heart of Mary. She fell in love with the many liturgical services which offered her an opportunity to play different musical scores. I was thrilled when she and her daughter, Carolyn, entered our Rite of Christian Initiation for Adults to learn the Catholic Church tradition in preparation for becoming a Catholic. I considered it a blessing to welcome them into the Catholic Church at the Easter Vigil service. There was great rejoicing in our parish family that Easter when the two Carolyns and Andrew, Mrs. Smoke's son, became full-fledged members of Most Pure Heart of Mary Church.

Carolyn didn't stop there; she went on to study the liturgy of the Catholic Church at Springhill College in Mobile. She is now versed in Catholic liturgy and is a professional gospel choir musician whose services are requested at the Cathedral and throughout Mobile.

I used all the talent and resources at my disposal to establish an active Parish Council and Finance Committee. Once on its feet, the Parish Council addressed the many needs of the parish and served well to support me in the administration of the parish.

During the course of my four years at Most Pure Heart of Mary Parish, my mom and dad's medical conditions deteriorated. On April 28, 1989, my Sister Carolyn, gave up her apartment and job as a registered nurse in New York City to return to Pascagoula and provide home health care for our parents. She was indeed a God-send to our parents and her siblings who had great concern for their care. Carolyn lovingly provided the highest level of professional care for our parents for over ten years, most of which, one or both of them were bed-ridden. When either of our parents had to be admitted to the hospital, the doctor refused to let them stay there any longer than necessary. He affirmed what everyone in our family knew, "they got better nursing care at home".

While at Heart of Mary, I acquired certification to serve as a Chaplain at Keesler Airforce Base in Biloxi in order to provide needed additional financial support for my parents. On my day off, I traveled sixty-five miles each way to Biloxi and back to fulfill my responsibilities in that position. I really enjoyed my ministry at Keesler. It gave me the opportunity to not only administer the Sacraments but also to meet many fine people.

When Archbishop Lipscomb learned that I was working at Keesler, he called me in to inquire why. I told him that I needed to help provide financial support for my parents. He actually thanked me for doing that. He then asked how much I was making as a Chaplain. When I told him, he responded by putting me on the archdiocesan payroll and replacing that salary each month. He preferred that I remain available to my parishioners rather than work at Keesler. I will always be grateful for his compassion and support.

One Sunday morning, during the middle of winter, I opened the church to find out that the heating system was not working. I conscientiously asked the parishioners for money to purchase a new unit. They out rightly told me "no". They wanted me to go north to beg for the money which I refused to do. This was an expectation peculiar to some of our southern parishes. Most of the schools and parishes that the Josephites had established along the Gulf Coast, were established in the early 1900s with the financial sponsorship of white Catholics from the north. (My own education through the seminary was subsidized with an endowment from Captain and Mrs. William Boone in Baltimore.) St. Katherine Drexel, an heiress from Philadelphia, used her substantial inheritance to establish a number of schools in the south to educate Black children. The practice of having pastors beg for financial support for black Catholic parishes in the south was still an expectation in many parishes. I was working to empower my parishioners to determine their own destiny by financially supporting their own endeavors and churches.

My refusal to go north and beg, was not received well and one of the negative vestiges of our shared heritage, distrust, began to show its ugly head. Because of my refusal, the parishioners let me know that they did not want a black pastor.

Pained by their response, I requested a transfer from the parish. I knew that there were other Josephites parishes that would welcome a black pastor. I later learned that the pervasive attitude of the parishioners was: "Don't worry; he is not going anywhere because he is taking care of his parents in Pascagoula". Needless to say, they were shocked when I told them I had been transferred to St. Francis Xavier Parish in Baton Rouge, Louisiana. I also informed them that their new pastor (a Caucasian) would assume pastoral responsibility in a couple of days. When the time came for me to leave, they told me, "Sister Marianna stays with us." My response was, "No way!"

I have reason to believe that several of the parishioners at Heart of Mary also thought that I was supporting my parents from the parish coffers and had spread that untruth. They did not know that Archbishop Lipscomb had put me on his parole. The financial records for the parish were left balanced and in order.

A footnote to this experience is that, twenty years later, when I was elected Superior General, Heart of Mary was the first parish that called and asked me to speak at their Annual Prayer Breakfast. I accepted, and they used this opportunity to apologize for the way they responded to me and confessed that they had not been ready to appreciate and support a black pastor at the time. They went on to say that they had experienced a change of heart. In 2013, as Superior General, I sent them an African Josephite to be their pastor. They embraced him with love and have supported him in restoring the church, repairing the leak in the bell tower (which had been there for many years), and in converting the convent into the rectory with a chapel for daily Mass. The Lord continues to work in His own time.

CHAPTER 10

— ✤ —

Praise Him in Song

and Dance

"This Little Light of Mine"

ON OCTOBER 1, 1991, I enjoyed the two-hour drive from Mobile to my new assignment at St. Francis Xavier Parish. St. Francis Xavier Parish was a wonderful parish community blessed with a beautiful church and was effectively serving the spiritual needs of parishioners. They also had a good but very traditional choir. Of course, I again went about establishing a gospel choir and introducing Black spirituality to the liturgy. The response of the parishioners was one of cautious acceptance. I found a temporary African American music director, Mr. Donovan Rosette, who was a skilled professional music and choir director.

One of the happiest memories of my first year in Baton Rouge was observing Mr. Rosette's skillful training of our choir for a Christmas Cantata. Listening to the nearly forty-member choir singing in four-part harmony was truly moving and brought joy to my heart. At Mr. Rosette's request, I hired members of the Baton Rouge Symphony Orchestra to play with the choir for the Cantata.

I secured St. Joseph Cathedral for the Cantata performance. The Cathedral was filled with parishioners and friends from throughout Baton Rouge. The Master of Ceremony was, Kim Hunter, an African American newscaster from the local TV station. The Cantata was a big hit and I could not have been more pleased. St. Francis Xavier parishioners were indeed blessed that Christmas.

Permanent leadership of the gospel choir was established under the direction of Mrs. Patricia Armstrong. The choir quickly distinguished itself at the Sunday Mass and we soon had a full church at each gospel Mass. The worshippers liked what they heard and were delighted to be able to celebrate their rich cultural heritage in the Catholic Church. May God be ever praised!

I included the teens and young adults in the parish liturgy by establishing a liturgical dance group which we named Sacred Dancers. They danced with grace and reverence, moving in step with the smooth rhythms of the spirituals and gospel music. The parishioners were moved and delighted whenever they performed their liturgical ministry at Mass. Mrs. Brigette Richard still directs the liturgical dancers at St. Francis Xavier. I was thrilled as Superior General to accept their invitation to preside at the Mass celebrating the Silver Jubilee of the Sacred Dancers.

St. Francis Xavier Parish had a thriving elementary school staffed by the Sisters of the Holy Family. It was a joy to teach the students about Black culture and history in the Catholic Church. It was empowering for them to learn about Black saints and the contributions that they have made to church doctrine. They displayed their new knowledge with great pride in song and in the performing arts. They were proud to be black and Catholic.

When the time came for me to hire another principal for the school, I hired a retired teacher and parishioner, Mrs. Lorena Turner. Under her administration, the academic standard of the school improved and financial support for the school increased. Mrs. Turner was a God-send and remains a good friend of mine!

Sister Marianna followed me to St. Francis Xavier where she lived with the Holy Family Sisters. Once again, she won the love and support of the parishioners through her ministry to the needy: caring for the sick and home-bound and engaging them in a ministry of prayer for the parish. We both still maintain contact with several of the parishioners at St. Francis Xavier.

My call to leadership development in the parish was received enthusiasti-cally. I set up workshops to train lectors, altar servers, Parish Council mem-bers, Eucharistic Ministers, and leaders for parish initiatives. As a result of the work that I had done with the liturgy over the years, while at St Francis, I was asked to write an article on the African American Parish for the New Theology Review, An American Catholic Journal for Ministry

My service at St. Francis Xavier Parish was happy and spiritually fulfilling. Even though I was aware that a cadre of strong parishioners (mostly Creoles whose families had been members of the parish for many generations) did not want a black pastor, I continued to work for their recognition and respect. This group fought me at every turn as I tried to implement Black spirituality in the liturgy. Many years later at the 25th anniversary celebration of the liturgical dance group, it was clear that they had grown to appreciate the cultural ele-ments of the liturgy.

CHAPTER 11

The "Mother Church" of Black Catholics

"Blessed Assurance"

AFTER FIVE YEARS at St. Francis Xavier, my Superior, Father Kearns, asked me to consider a transfer to St. Francis Xavier Parish in Baltimore, the "Mother Church" for Black Catholics in the United States. I was greatly confused by this change so I asked him why? He told me that he wanted me to help the parish eliminate its debt and strengthen its pastoral ministry. After two weeks, I consented and began making my way once again to "Charm City".

I drove to Baltimore from the "Red Stick" (Baton Rouge). When I arrived on September 27, 1996, I was welcomed by Mitzy Willis, the parish secretary. I really felt honored to assume the pastoral administration of historic St. Francis Xavier Parish, founded in 1863 and served by the Josephites since 1871. Under the powerful pastoral leadership of Fr. Henry Offer, S.S.J., it had a rich history of fruitful ministry implementing African American spirituality. Father Offer was a Caucasian who was miles ahead of many of his Josephite confreres in implementing Black spirituality, culture and history in the parish. Short in stature, he humbly accepted the criticism of some of the local priests for doing this. In spite of this, he did what he felt the Lord was calling him to do with conviction and pride.

I began my tenure there by working with the choir director to coordinate hymn selections for Mass with the scriptural readings of the liturgy. The cultivation of Black leadership was the pastoral demand that consumed most of my energy. Unlike the other parishes that I has served, the parishioners of St. Francis Xavier were proud that they were black and Catholic and they were proud of their legacy of being the "Mother Church of Black Catholics" in the United States. My job was to convince them that pride in being black should include taking ownership of the parish by assuming financial responsibility and eliminating the debt.

The parish was heavily indebted to the Archdiocese and was notorious for not paying the Archbishop's Annual Appeal. They responded positively to my challenge and worked diligently to pay off the debt. In 1998, for the first time in many years, St. Francis Xavier was freed of its indebtedness to the archdiocese. When the archbishop came to a dinner at the Josephite headquarters, he was eager to find out how I had done it. I explained to him the process I used to empower the people and develop their pride, leadership, and sense of ownership for the parish.

Once the debt was paid, my attention focused on restoring the interior of the four-story rectory. I hired a member of the parish, a contractor, to paint, put up wall paper and refinish the wood floors. The kitchen was renovated and a new dining room set and beds were purchased. For the first time in many years, the rectory appeared fresh and welcoming.

The brilliant and esteemed Father Joseph Verrett, who mentored me in the seminary, was residing in the rectory. He became one of my best friends, supporting my every effort to strengthen leadership in the parish by means of the Parish Council, Finance Committee and other parish organizations. When he perceived that I needed a break, he took me away from the parish for a leisurely dinner.

In addition to serving as pastor of St. Francis Xavier, I served as Pastoral Director for our seminarians at St. Joseph Seminary in D. C. I was responsible for assigning the seminarians to assist in various parishes on Sundays by teaching religion or helping wherever necessary.

In May of 1997, I had the privilege of offering the prayer at the public ceremony where Secretary Alexis Herman was sworn into office by Vice President Al Gore as the first African American Secretary of Labor. Secretary Herman was trained in Josephite parishes and schools in Mobile, Alabama. Alexis and my sister, Paulette, are life-long friends. She, Paulette, and Marion (Paulette's husband) were classmates at Most Pure Heart of Mary High School.

I really enjoyed my ministry at St. Francis Xavier. The parishioners were very supportive and responsive to my leadership. They fell in love with Sister Marianna and were inspired by her ministry to the sick and shut-in, her outreach to the needy in the community and her friendly visits to the homes of parishioners.

In 1999, Father Kearns, surfaced again with another request of me. This time he asked me to go to Nigeria for a couple of months and spend time on the compound of the Missionaries of St. Paul (M.S.P.) in Iperu-Remo. He wanted me to observe and take note of their formation program for new aspirants and draw up a sketch for a Josephite house of formation to be built on the M.S.P. compound.

I left St. Francis Xavier to spend several months between each of the M.S.P. seminaries in Iperu-Remo and Abuja. When I returned to the States, I was invited to a General Council meeting to share my observations and present my sketch of a potential Josephite house of formation. The Council was very pleased with the information and presentation. When I finished, I excused myself. I was eager to get back to my parish, St. Francis Xavier. Before I could get out of the door, the Superior stopped me and asked: "Bill, who do you think should build this formation house and begin the program there for the Josephites?" "I don't know" I said. "That's a decision that the Council should make". He said: "Bill, we want you to do that." In total disbelief, I sat down again and asked: "Why me?" He remarked that I seemed to like Africa and Nigeria. "You have gone there several summers for your vacation." I couldn't deny that I had enjoyed my time in Nigeria. After a moment of prayerful consideration, I told him that I would go. The Lord had blindsided me once again.

The decision to go to Africa meant that I would need to permanently terminate my pastoral ministry at St. Francis Xavier Parish. I had grown to love the parishioners most dearly so, saying goodbye was very difficult. Because I knew that the Josephites desperately needed to increase its membership in order to serve the African American community in the future, I was willing to make the sacrifice. The parishioners sent me off with their blessing. In my heart, I felt that Jesus, my good Shephard, was going with me and that He would add success to the work of my hands. Father Gervase Mbanude, a M.S.P. priest and my associate, assumed the pastoral responsibilities at St. Francis Xavier Parish.

CHAPTER 12

Building the Future

"In Christ There is No East or West"

PRIOR TO GOING to Nigeria, I spent time in Atlanta with my sister, Paulette, and her husband, Marion. I was always welcomed by the parishioners and pastors at their parish, St. Anthony of Padua Catholic Church, and was often invited to make comments. When I told the congregation about my new assignment and the challenges I would face in Nigeria, the Men's Club (in which Marion was a leader) decided to help. They raised money to help purchase computers, kitchen supplies and the water purification tower that I needed to have installed. I will always be grateful for their support and encouragement. I continue to visit St. Anthony whenever I go to Atlanta.

In the spirit of a true missionary, I left Baltimore for Lagos, Nigeria on June 6, 1999. I was picked up at Murtala Muhammed International Airport by several M.S.P. priests. After gathering my many bags that included canned food and other comfort items that my sisters insisted I bring, we traveled the fifty miles to the seminary in Iperu-Remo. I was given a room at the end of the visitor's quarters near St. Mark's student dormitory and began to feather my nest.

Getting Started

The M.S.P. priests stationed on the compound were suspicious of my presence. Apparently, Fr. Kearns had not adequately paved the way for my mission or it had not been properly communicated by the M.S.P. Superior to the rest of the priests. They thought I had come to take over their formation program. I spent several weeks trying to convince them that my only purpose was to learn from them the details of operating a house of spiritual formation for potential Josephite candidates.

Eventually, I was able to allay their fears and assure them that I would work in collaboration with them to form Josephite and St. Paul candidates for entrance into St. Paul seminaries in Iperu-Remo and Abuja. A team of formators was assembled to work for the well-being of both religious communities. I taught English, liturgy and religion and served as a Spiritual Director. I lived in community with the M.S.P. priests, eating, praying and socializing with them.

On Sundays, I celebrated Mass with the M.S.P.'s in St. Paul Chapel on the compound. In addition to the seminarians, many local people also attended Mass at St. Paul. On the weekends, I often traveled to Lagos or to either of the two federal schools to offer Mass or administer the Sacrament of Reconciliation. Hearing confessions at St. Charles Church in Lagos was an unbelievable experience. It was not unusual for me to be in the confessional for three or four hours because of the number of people who came. It was humbling and inspiring to see and experience the profound faith of the Nigerian people.

As I went back and forth to Lagos and traveled through Iperu-Remo, I could not help but notice the conditions and dismal learning environment of the schools. Students in the local public school in Iperu-Remo where desperately trying to learn without pens, pencils, paper or other essential learning materials. Whenever I returned to Africa from the States, many people gave me supplies that I could use in the seminary or that I could share with the local people. The parishioners of St. Anthony of Padua in Atlanta usually made contributions and Mrs. Julia Matthews of Baltimore always gave me $500 when I returned. I used this money to help purchase books, pencils, paper and other supplies for the children attending public schools in Iperu. The parents, students and teachers were always so very grateful for the help.

Having taken my place in the formation program, I began making plans to construct a Josephite House of Formation at the far end of the compound. The area allotted to us was heavily covered with weeds. It also had an abandoned chicken coup, a massive bamboo tree (a habitat for cobras), and a lot of trash on it. I hired a crew of men to begin cleaning and clearing the land for construction.

Soon after getting started, I hired Godwin Urama to be my driver. This sounds like a luxury but believe me it was essential. Driving in Nigeria was dangerous on several levels. Many of the roads were unpaved and crowded with aggressive drivers in old mini-vans and cars. It was not unusual to be stopped on the highway by police with machine guns, people peddling small wares (i.e., ice, bread, coat hangers), or bandits with machetes. Periodically dangerous tribal rituals were in effect of which I had no awareness. In addition, I was considered an elder and not expected to drive. Godwin knew how to navigate the roads, spoke the language, and knew the culture. He was not only a safety net but also a trusted companion.

Building the House of Spiritual Formation

In the meantime, Father Augustine Inwang, M.S.P. helped me to secure Mr. Emma Alwerioghene, a construction engineer and architect from Benin City. Mr. Alwerioghene had made a name for himself constructing a school for the Jesuits. He, in turn, hired an Italian building contractor out of Lagos, Cappa & D'Alberto, to do the work. Construction began with the hiring of local workers who leveled the lot by manually excavating it in the scorching sun. No machines were used.

Father Kearns gave the sketches that I had made to a construction company in Baltimore and blueprints were drawn up for the new St. Joseph House of Spiritual Formation. Construction began as soon as Cappa & D'Alberto received the documents. I was totally involved in the project for the nine months that it took to complete it.

In addition to being project manager for the construction, I taught, served as the Josephite Vocation Director and was responsible for selecting the "pioneer" group of Nigerian seminarians. When word spread that the Josephites were accepting candidates to study for the priesthood, a steady stream of young men came from far and wide seeking admittance. Interviewing became almost a full-time job in itself. Unfortunately, we could only select ten from the more than one hundred that came. I was working day and night but I loved every minute of it.

Father Augustine helped me to establish banking services at Oceanic Bank in Lagos where finances for the construction were periodically wired to me. Each banking transmittal consumed an entire day of my time waiting for bankers to sign countless books to document the transfer. The bankers moved at their own pace, and that was slow, slow, and slower! When the transaction was finally completed, I was anxious to get a bite to eat and a cold Star beer before being driven the fifty miles back to the compound. This was no easy trip—the roads were treacherous not only because of the reckless driving and road conditions but also because of the constant threat of bandits along the route.

As if all of this were not enough, I received a call on March 30, 1999 that my mother had passed away. I was devastated. I prepared to return to the States to preside over her funeral. The telephone system in Iperu-Remo went out immediately after the initial call from my sister, Paulette. I was not able to reach her again to let my family know when I would arrive in Pascagoula. The Superior immediately had arrangements made for my travel and informed my family.

My mother's funeral was a beautiful "home going" service. Bishop Joseph Howze, Ordinary of Biloxi, and over fifteen Josephite priests concelebrated the Mass with me. Family and friends, including Secretary Alexis Herman and Mrs. Coretta Scott King, came from near and far to provide support and comfort to us. She was a beautiful woman and mother. My father had passed away five years earlier, just one month shy of their sixtieth wedding anniversary. He became paralyzed after surgery on his neck, was bedridden and suffered for five years before he passed. After each of my parents died, we heard wonderful stories from family, neighbors, and sometimes, even people we had never met, about their many quiet acts of generosity and charity. I miss them both dearly but I know that they are with our Lord and Savior.

In August of 1999, I selected ten candidates to study in the Josephite Formation Program. Because our facility was still under construction, they resided at St. Mark Residence with the M.S.P. candidates. The Josephite candidates prayed, studied, recreated and ate with the M.S.P.'s. They became a family that would someday work together as priests in the United States. In the evenings and sometimes during the day, I shared with them the history of the Society of St. Joseph and taught them African American History.

The Josephite House of Spiritual Formation gradually emerged from the hard Nigerian soil. I hired Nelson Woodwork, a furniture company in Benin, to make beds, tables, chairs, cabinets, desks, the altar, and sanctuary furniture for the house. I purchased a stove, refrigerators, freezer, washing machine, generator, transformer, a water treatment plant, and air conditioners for the staff rooms. I also hired a seamstress to make curtains for the bedrooms, classrooms, library, and community room.

As the construction scaffolding and equipment were moved from the property, I hired a landscaper to plant appropriate shrubbery in the front of the new building. As May 6, 2000, approached, I sent invitations to friends and to the other religious houses nearby to join us for the Dedication Mass. May 6th was the date of my parents' wedding anniversary. I knew that they would be with me the entire day.

Wouldn't you know it, two weeks before the dedication I was hospitalized at Sacred Heart Hospital, in Abeokuta, thirty-five miles from Iperu-Remo. I had a severe case of cellulitis which left me unable to walk. At 65 years old, this was the first time I had ever been admitted into a hospital. I was anxious to return to the compound to finish my work and take care of all the remaining details for the dedication.

Five days before the dedication, a Pakistani female doctor concerned that I was not healing, studied my chart and determined that I was receiving the wrong antibiotics. She ordered stronger antibiotics for me which immediately stopped the pain and put me back on my feet. I returned to the compound a couple days before the dedication and worked like a beaver to get everything in place for the big day. Between the strenuous work schedule, the extreme heat, the Nigerian diet, and my illness, I had lost twenty-five pounds by the time of the dedication.

I anxiously awaited the arrival of my sisters and brother-in-law: Kirt, Paulette, and Marion, as well as Sisters Lois Davis and Marianna of the Sisters of Social Service. Four parishioners from Sts. Francis Xavier and St. Peter Claver Parishes in Baltimore also came for the dedication.

During the days before the dedication, Marion worked with our new cook, Thomas, to teach him how to make a few American dishes (including gumbo) so that I could have more nutritious and tasty meals. I had grown quite weary of the daily diet of rice with tomato sauce, fish and cassava. Fish is not one of my favorite foods. Marion brought spices with him from the States and he and Paulette prepared several tasty dishes. Paulette made a birthday cake for one of the candidates and we all sang "Happy Birthday" to him when the cake was served after dinner. This was a new experience for the young men that I has already initiated. I had a cake and decorated for each birthday. They enjoyed this special attention very much and still use the birthday banners that I hung when I was there.

Marion and Paulette worked well together in the kitchen. The men around the compound noticed and commented that they would tell their wives of the American man who helped his wife in the kitchen. Thomas soon honed his skills and eventually became a master. He made some of the best corn bread and shrimp creole that I have ever tasted! After I left Nigeria, he was able to secure a job with a wealthy couple in Lagos.

Marion, who was trained as a musician, also worked with our Josephite candidates to teach them a couple of gospel songs. It was initially difficult for them to relate to the emotional energy of gospel songs because they did not have the same historical experience of African Americans. Once Marion talked to them about the freedom struggle of African Americans and their attachment to Jesus as their savior and liberator, they began to better understand the emotional foundation of the song. They, in turn, taught Marion a few African songs which he took back with him to St. Anthony.

Father Robert Kearns, our Superior General, arrived for the dedication and was totally surprised by the beauty of the house, its solid construction and its beautiful and well-appointed interior. Bishop Albert Fasina, the Ordinary of the Diocese of Ijebu-Odi, also arrived and was delighted to see the beautiful facility that had been built. He was honored to have been asked to celebrate the Mass and bless the new St. Joseph the Worker House of Spiritual Formation.

May 6, 2000 was a hot but glorious day! Because the chapel was too small to accommodate the large crowd anticipated, we placed the altar on the front porch at the entrance of the house and placed chairs for our guests under the large tent which had been erected on the front lawn. The seminarians were well prepared and eager to provide music for the occasion. We were blessed by the presence of several of the candidates' parents, many of our Sunday worshippers, friends of the Josephites and Missionaries of St. Paul. Several of our guests brought live chickens and other gifts for the occasion. Representatives of all the religious communities in the area also joined us.

The dedication ceremony was impressive and reverently performed by Bishop Fasina. He blessed every room of the facility with holy water and consecrated the altar for the celebration of Holy Mass. There were more than a hundred-fifty people in attendance including approximately twenty-five priests.

After Mass, we spread throughout the house to await a delicious meal followed by African music and dancing in the yard to crown off a wonderful day of celebration. Father Kearns happily received many accolades for the construction of the House of Formation. The Missionaries of St. Patrick told him that they had never built a house of formation as beautifully designed as this one or in as short a period of time as this one built by Father Bill.

Through Dangers, Toils and Snares

Our students had already moved into their new rooms with showers and toilets shared by two students. Even though electricity, hot water and telephone access was spotty, at best, we all felt that we were living in luxury with clean beds, good food and space to study, pray, and recreate. Visiting Nigeria is one thing but living there is another. The intense heat and humidity, mosquitoes, snakes, spotty electricity, lack of hot water, the rainy season and other threats to personal safety made the experience constantly challenging. Our new house offered shelter from most of these realities of life.

When I built our House of Formation, I had it constructed with steel doors at every entrance. Each day at the conclusion of evening prayer, the doors were locked to prevent robbers from entering. We all felt very safe and secure. One day after the doors were locked, I was in a discussion with four of the seminarians in my suite when four robbers with guns barged into my room demanding money and all of my personal possessions. The robbers had gained access to the main building by means of the cook who lived in a separate building. They knew that he would have a key so they went to him and forced him to let them in.

Father Jim McLinden, our Nigerian Vocation Director, had just returned to the States. Before he left, I had given him money to pay for the travel of the young men who had been accepted as Josephite candidates. After paying for their travel, Fr. Jim had two hundred dollars left which he returned to me. That money was in my desk so I gave it to them. They also took my camera, computer and watch.

They brought the cook back to my office where I was still being held with the four seminarians. Speaking in Yoruba, one of the robbers told the others that he wanted to kill us. One of the seminarians who also spoke Yoruba understood what he said and told me. The other bandits told the blood-thirsty one that they had not come to kill anyone, only to get our possessions and money. I was, of course alarmed and afraid, but I was most concerned about the seminarians, especially those who were still in their rooms.

The robbers continued to search every area of my suite for additional money but found none. I had hidden several hundred dollars for staff salaries and food for the month behind my cassock in the closet. They looked into the closet but did not find the money because they did not remove my cassock. Frustrated, the leader decided to lock us in my bathroom. He then locked my bedroom door and the door of my office before finally leaving. We remained there for an hour until I felt sure that the robbers were gone. During the robbery, the perpetrators asked the whereabouts of the other seminarians. I immediately became more alarmed fearing that they would be found and hurt. One of the seminarians thought quickly and told them that the other seminarians had gone home. Thank goodness they did not bother to check. We prayed that they would not emerge from the cloistered living quarters but one of them did. Before he was seen however, he was able to quickly assess what was happening and quietly returned to tell the other seminarians. All of them immediately hid under their beds. They understood the danger of the situation better than I did. They remained under their beds for more than an hour. Finally one of them got the courage to come and peek down the corridor to see what was happening.

I had worked my way through the bathroom door and bedroom door but I was unable to unlock the door to my office door to free us completely. When I realized that one of the seminarians was lurking in the corridor, I yelled to him to come and let us out. He was too frightened to expose himself. The seminarians who were locked in with me were also afraid that the robbers might still be around so they begged me to lower my voice. I told them that we had been there for more than an hour and that I was sure the intruders had left by now.

I continued to shout for help but the Missionaries of St. Paul were too far away to hear my call of distress. Finally, the other seminarians got enough courage to come to our aid. I asked them to look for the key which I suspected the robbers had thrown on the floor. They looked, but did not see it. I then told them to go to the storage room and get the sledge hammer to break the door down. As soon as the door was breached, I exited the office and found the key lying on the floor in the corner of the corridor. The young men were so afraid that they had overlooked it.

We notified the Missionaries of St. Paul who were housed at the other end of the compound. They called the police who got a full report from me and told me that they would be on the lookout for the robbers. Soon after, representatives of the Muslim community came and asked me not to consider leaving their community because of this incident. They appreciated the presence of the Josephites because we provided jobs for several people in the community. They told me that they would engage the vigilante and, if anyone in the community had robbed us, they would take care of it. A month later, they came to inform me that the robbery was not done by anyone in the community. The band of robbers had been on a spree, robbing churches in Ijebu-Odi. The vigilante had caught them and "took care of them". I did not ask how but, knowing the culture, I was sure it involved great violence.

Building Community

During the Christmas and Easter holidays, I encouraged the first year candidates to select a novel from our library (which I named in honor of Father Slattery, our first Superior General) to read and write a book report to be presented on the first day of class. I did this not only to provide reading pleasure for them but also help familiarize them with American culture, sentence structure, and grammar.

I returned to the States at least yearly during the first few years. Before I returned to Iperu for the third year, I jokingly asked Sister Charlotte Marshall,

O.S.P. (who was principal at St. Benedict the Moor School when I was pastor) if she would go with me to Nigeria to teach American English to our students. She responded without hesitation with a resounding "Yes". "What do I need to do to prepare to go?" Sister Charlotte was in her eighties but she still had a missionary spirit. She accompanied me to Nigeria and I gave her the room inscribed in honor of Mother Mary Lange, Foundress of the Oblate Sisters of Providence.

As Sister Charlotte was settling in with her classes, she encountered a bit of stubbornness from the students when she tried to have them use American English and pronunciation instead of the British-style. She eventually convinced them that if they wanted to work effectively with African Americans, they would have to speak American English to be understood. Once she finally convinced them, Sister Charlotte's class became one of the favorite classes in the curriculum. They even wanted to take her with them to St. Paul Seminary, in Abuja.

I must share an amusing incident that occurred with Sr. Charlotte. Our local Ordinary, Bishop Fasina, gave the Josephites a ram. The ram became Sister Charlotte's constant companion. It roamed the compound with her wherever she went. On a beautiful Sunday morning while I was celebrating Mass, Sister Charlotte glimpsed out of the chapel window and caught sight of my dog, Daisy, chasing the ram. Within seconds, the ram sought safety by crashing through the chapel window and into Sr. Charlotte's lap. Needless to say, Sr. Charlotte jumped up in fright and confusion. I had to stop the Mass to wipe away my tears of laughter! I have never let her forget her encounter with the Catholic ram on Sunday morning. After that, she had the ram locked up. She did not see it again until the seminarians served it to her on a platter. She, of course, refused to partake.

During the Christmas and Easter breaks, we took the candidates for a swim and a picnic on the shore of the Atlantic Ocean and to Abeokuta to climb Oluma Rock. While in Abeokuta, we took the opportunity to visit Bishop Alfred Adewale Martins, the Ordinary of the Diocese.

Our candidates loved to play soccer which helped to keep them physically fit and spiritually robust. On recreation days, they inevitably chose sides and played soccer until the end of the recreation period. Their games with one another were great practice for the quarterly games they played with the students at the houses of formation in Ijebu-Odi and Ibadan. They greatly looked forward to competing with the other seminarians.

One of the most memorable experiences that I had occurred during my visit to the home of one of our candidates, Xavier Edet, in East Nigeria. Before I left on the trip, Xavier told me that I would need a letter from him to present to his parents when I arrived. He handed me a letter and a photo of himself in his white soutane (clerical cassock) to show to his family. He was sure that when they saw me they would assume that he was dead. I chuckled suspecting that he only wanted me to be his mailman.

When I arrived at the Edet home, Mrs. Edet met me at the door. I told her who I was and, lo and behold, she immediately asked when had her son died! I tried to assure her that Xavier was not dead but she sent a family member anyway to notify her husband (who was working in the fields) and all of the relatives in the compound, that her son was dead. I quickly withdrew the letter and photo from my pocket and gave them to her. She calmed down and shared the letter with her husband and the other members of the family who had just arrived. They let me know that a "white" man (there is no word in the language for "African American" so, I am described as "white"), coming to their home in reference to their son, would normally only mean that I was bringing them the sad news of his death. Finally convinced that their son was alive, they welcomed Godwin Urama and me as guests and provided us with food and drink.

On our way to the Edet home in Owerri, we stopped at Godwin's home in Enugu to visit his mom and siblings. Godwin had already told his mom about me so, she was delighted to finally meet me and welcomed me to her home. One of the things that Godwin had told her was that I liked cashews. She had gathered a large bag of the delicious nuts from her back yard, packaged them, and had them ready for to me to take back with me. To my surprise, she not only gave me cashews, she gave me her son. She said to me: "Godwin's father is deceased so, from now on, you are his father." No one was happier than Godwin himself. Over the years, I have officiated at his wedding at St. John Vienney Parish in Iperu-Remo, rejoiced with him and his wife, Grace, at their wedding reception held at St. Joseph the Worker House of Spiritual Formation, and baptized their first child. One of their daughters was named after my sister, Kirticina. Godwin and I have remained very close--he is indeed "my son". During the time that he served as my driver, he participated in Masses and community prayer with the candidates and shared community life in every way. The Lord works in mysterious ways!

While in Iperu-Remo, I inadvertently became instrumental in the establishment of Immaculate Conception Church after Mr. and Mrs. Alexander asked me to offer Sunday Mass in their home. Although the Alexanders normally attended Mass at St. Paul Chapel on the seminary compound, they continued to request that I offer Mass in their home. Once I started offering Mass in their home, the number of people who came increased each week. Eventually, so many people came for Mass that we had to move it from the Alexander home to the nearby parking lot and then to a place across the Lagos-Shagamu Highway. This gathering ultimately became an out-mission of St. Anthony Church in Shagamu. I was able to provide a great portion of the money to help the group begin a new parish which they named Immaculate Conception. Though it is still incomplete, it is currently being used as a parish church and a M.S.P. priest serves as the pastor.

Two Steps Forward, One Step Back

As the years progressed and our seminarians completed their study of philosophy at the M.S.P.'s St. Paul Seminary in Abuja, they returned to the Josephite House of Formation to await arrangements to be made for their travel to the United States. The American Immigration Office in Lagos became a stone wall that eventually put a stop to our acceptance of future candidates. The American

Embassy denied visas to two entire classes! These students came to me utterly frustrated. Though I was working as hard as I could to break through the wall, they did not believe that I was doing enough to get them to the States. The 911 terrorist attack in New York two years earlier as well as the increase of African immigrants engaged in illegal drugs, scams, and other crimes in the States, had brought intense scrutiny to the immigration of young Africans, particularly males, to the United States.

Eventually, I sent some of the seminarians to the French Village in Badagry in Lagos to study French and later on to the Formation House of the Society of African Missions (SMA), in Ibadan. They studied at Sts. Peter and Paul Seminary while in Ibadan. They were welcomed at both places. As an added benefit, our excellent soccer players helped the S.M.A. seminarians end their losing streak in soccer.

Because of the problems we continued to have with the American Embassy, the Superior, Father Kearns, terminated our formation program at Iperu-Remo before he left office.

I returned to the United States in the spring of 2004 with mixed emotions. On the one hand, I clearly understood that we couldn't continue to house the Josephite seminarians who had completed their philosophy curriculum, however, I also did not want to close the house and discontinue the intake of candidates. We had worked so hard to build a beautiful facility and a solid program of spiritual development. The candidates were now ready and willing to continue their training in the States and embrace the Josephite mission to serve African Americans. It was quite an investment on the part of the Josephites not to be able to now reap all of the benefits.

My ministry at the House of Formation took me to the pinnacle of my service as a Josephite priest. I sincerely felt I was fulfilling a portion of the dream of our first Superior, Father John Slattery, who longed to welcome Blacks into our Society to minister to our African American parishioners. I was commissioned to be the first formator of our Nigerian candidates. It was my distinct privilege to introduce them to the Society of St. Joseph, our African American spirituality, culture, and history and to an appreciation of the American Catholic Church. It was my joy to see them grow spiritually and to live in community with them. Hearing their voices singing the Holy Office of the Church in harmony each day, was truly a beautiful and uplifting experience!

The great majority of Josephite priests were now over 60 years of age, some were retiring due to sickness and others would go to their eternal reward within the next five to ten years. Consequently, I saw these young men not only as future priests but as the future of the Josephites--those who would sustain the Josephite mission of evangelization in the African American community.

Finally, Father Edward Chiffriller, the new Superior General, and I made an appointment with the American Ambassador who gave us a mild apology and then processed our candidates to go to America. All was not lost. The candidates who had completed their studies in Nigeria between 2000 and 2005 were eventually given visas to come to the United States.

Some in our community did not agree with the recruitment of Nigerians for the Josephite ministry. They did not accept the fact that we were no longer getting vocations from our parishes nor did they have a solution for our declining numbers. They did not seem to recall that the original Josephites were not America either. They were Italian or Irish Catholics. There was no difference. It is a tribute to Father Kearns and the General Council at the time that a decision was made to recruit from the bounty of God's vineyard.

During the time that I was in Nigeria, I was able to select and spiritually prepare twenty-five Nigerian men to become Josephite seminarians. Twenty-one of them continued their studies at St. Joseph Seminary in Washington, D.C. and all twenty-one have been ordained as priests. As Superior General, I had the great honor of appointing some of the Nigerian Josephites to serve as pastors in our parishes and as teachers at St. Augustine High School. These young men are the future of the Josephite community. What a blessing for the Society and for me!

Nigeria

Seminarians in Iperu-Remo, Nigeria

St. Joseph House of Spiritual Formation,
Iperu-Remo, Nigeria

Fr. Kearns who sent me to establish
the house of spiritual formation

Sr. Charlotte and me with seminarians

Bishop Fasina and Fr. Kearns blessing the residence in Iperu-Remo

Marion teaching the seminarians gospel songs

Holding my godson, William,
son of Eddie Onah

Godwin Urama, his wife,
Grace, and daughter, Peace

With public school children in Iperu-Remo

CHAPTER 13

— ❧ —

You Can't Go Home Again

"Lord Help Me to Hold Out"

IN OBEDIENCE, I boarded the return flight from Lagos to Baltimore in the summer of 2004. When I arrived, Father Chiffriller asked me if I would consider being pastor of my home parish, St. Peter the Apostle in Pascagoula. The pastor, Father Sullivan, had just died. Without hesitation, I said "yes". I looked upon the assignment as an opportunity to return thanks to the parish that had nurtured my vocation. It also meant that I would return home to be near my family, relatives and friends.

I arrived in Pascagoula on August 3, 2004 and immediately began to renew acquaintances and check out the condition of the parish campus facilities, including the school. The Norvel clan welcomed me back with opened arms and a small reception.

The Sisters of the Holy Spirit still staffed the school which was functioning but not self-sustaining. The rectory, church and school were all in need of minor repairs. Father Sullivan had saved enough money to make the necessary repairs so I proceeded to get them done at a cost of $36,000. When the repairs were complete, I paid and reinstated the lapsed property insurance policy.

Once the repairs were completed, I focused on developing leadership in the parish. I scheduled a leadership workshop for all of the leaders of the parish at the Divine Word Retreat Center in Bay Saint Louis, MS. I engaged the services of my brother-in-law, Marion (a professional trainer), and my sister, Paulette, to provide the training. The workshop progressed smoothly until we were forced to pay attention to the increasingly serious warnings of the approaching hurricane, Katrina. I terminated the workshop a bit early so that those participating could return to board up their homes. Paulette and Marion left immediately to return to Atlanta. After packing up our materials, I left the retreat center and drove the forty miles back to the rectory. I opted to travel on Highway 90 rather than Interstate 10 (I-10) because, by that time, I-10 was becoming congested with cars filled with people evacuating the area. It was a memorable journey: lights in the hotels, casinos, restaurants and novelty shops were all turned off. I had no inkling at that time, that it would be the last time I would see those buildings or the Biloxi Bridge. All of them were swallowed up by Katrina.

When I arrived at the rectory, I noticed that the water in the pond near the church had risen considerably. After unpacking, I dutifully prepared for Sunday Mass. When I woke up the next morning, the hurricane warnings were even more urgent. Countless people had already left the area for higher ground. When I completed my two morning Masses, I packed some clothing and a few possessions and, with my sister, Carolyn, joined the hundreds of people who were making their way north on I-10 and I-65. It was a slow and laborious journey--cars were bumper to bumper. We finally arrived in Atlanta on Sunday evening and made our way to the homes of our sisters, Paulette and Kirt.

Hurricane Katrina

On Sunday, August 29, 2005, Hurricane Katrina hit the Mississippi Gulf Coast with a savage blow, destroying everything in its path. We watched scenes of the tragic destruction on television. I became more and more anxious about what I would find when I returned to Pascagoula.

Three days after Katrina, I made my way back to my parish. The Highway Patrol would not allow cars to travel on I-10, so I used a back route and finally made it back to Pascagoula. What I saw of the city and my parish campus brought tears to my eyes. St. Peter's church had been hit by a tornado which totally destroyed its basic structure. In addition, all church furnishings and linens were ruined by the salt water. The rectory and convent, though not hit by the tornado, were water logged. All furnishings and appliances had to be discarded. My sister and I had to search for dry linens and a place to sleep. The box springs of the mattresses were wet and already smelled of mold.

Ten feet of water from the Gulf inundated many of the homes in the city; destroying some and leaving several feet of mud and debris in others. Any cars that were not used to evacuate were also destroyed by water. The immediate surge on the beach was said to have been twenty-eight feet! Very little was left standing within the first five or so blocks from the beach. Only remnants of homes and trees remained. Our family home, a mile from the beach, had at least four feet of water in it and the rectory, another mile further away, also sustained four feet of water that came from the nearby bay. There was no electricity, telephone service, grocery stores, restaurants, fresh water, gas or department stores available. Pascagoula was like a ghost town. It was devastating! The sun came out the next day as if nothing had happened and, with the heat, the mold immediately began to grow in the dry walls of the homes that remained standing.

Although the media focused on New Orleans, Katrina actually struck the Mississippi Gulf Coast. New Orleans was devastated by the breach of its levies, an unfortunate aftermath of the historic hurricane.

The day after we arrived back in Pascagoula, as Carolyn and I were removing debris from the rectory, my sister, Paulette, arrived from Atlanta with a generator, a battery operated radio, 30 gallons of gas, water, cleaning supplies, disinfectants, face masks, packaged food and cash! She also brought food which she had picked up in Montgomery from Kentucky fried chicken, which, for some reason, was still warm. She was a God-send.

The school which had served to educate our children for over a hundred years, was also destroyed by the tornado. Both the school and the church had to be completely razed. After a week or so, my cousin, Robert Norvel, a county official, had all the rubbish from the church and school removed from our parish grounds. This was a tremendous blessing for which we were very grateful. It would have cost the parish a great deal to get it removed by a private company.

The Red Cross provided us with hot food and water daily during the critical days that followed. A parishioner, Ms. Ruth McGee, gave me the use of her mother's home in Moss Point, only two miles away from the rectory. This became my new rectory. It was a tremendous relief to have a clean dry place to lay my head. My sister, Carolyn, cooked, helping to keep our bodies and souls together.

I was able to salvage enough chairs, tables, candles, a Sacramentary and Lectionary to set up a sacred space on the lawn to celebrate Sunday Mass for those parishioners who had returned to Pascagoula. My cousin, Robert, again helped by arranging to have some of the inmates from the prison across the street from the Church, help set up for Mass. They only requested that we reward their services with hamburgers and sodas. It was a time when neighbors helped neighbors in whatever way they could.

Tents which I purchased from Mobile, were erected for the celebration of Sunday Mass. The late fall and early winter eventually forced us to find a warmer place for our Eucharistic celebration. A parishioner, Mr. Tommy Molden, Principal of Magnolia Public School in Moss Point, graciously permitted us to celebrate Mass in the school auditorium.

Within the first couple of weeks after Katrina, Catholic church-groups from Illinois came to help re-build. They brought appliances, clothes, food and other supplies. Parishioners from St. Isadore Parish in Bloomingdale, Illinois came to our rescue by providing, not only money for the restoration of St. Peter's rectory and convent but also, supplies to restore the homes of some of our parishioners, including my sister, Carolyn. They refurnished the rectory and convent and purchased essential appliances. The electrical work, sheet rock, plumbing and carpentry were done by retired parishioners from St. Isadore Parish. They were, without a doubt, angels sent by God to demonstrate to us real Christian love in action – "You will know they are Christians by their love". They literally put St. Peter the Apostle parish back on its feet and on the road to recovery. They brought love, cheer, focus and helping hands in the midst of loss and confusion. After the restorations were complete, the pastor of St. Isadore, Father Tony Taschetta, and I exchanged pulpits for a Sunday Mass. I had an opportunity to thank the parishioners of St. Isadore and he was able to meet the people who had been served by them. We were all profoundly grateful for the generosity of St. Isadore Parish and will never forget the Christian charity that was extended to us.

Though grateful for the restoration of the rectory and convent, I dreaded the thought of constructing another church. The diocese had already determined that the school would not be rebuilt because there were not enough students to sustain it. As I sat in a bit of a trance on a remnant of the tornado-stricken church, I felt like Job sitting on his dung heap: discouraged and surrounded by destruction. As I was having my "pity party" and trying to decide what to do next, Father Michael Kelleher, Pastor of Sacred Heart Parish in south Pascagoula, drove up. He approached me and asked: "Bill, why are you just sitting there?!

I came to invite you to bring your parishioners to Sacred Heart for Sunday Mass. I will give you the 10 o'clock hour." In utter astonishment, I responded: "Mike, that's the time of your main Mass. Your parishioners will be very displeased." "I know. They will get over it," he said. I thanked him from the bottom of my heart and I will be eternally grateful for his profound generosity and charity in our time of need. He has continued to be a true friend to me.

We transported our piano and drums to Sacred Heart Church and, on the following Sunday, we celebrated our first Gospel Mass at Sacred Heart. Father Mike concelebrated with me as he did for every Mass thereafter. He loved our Gospel Mass.

As if that were not enough, he opened Sacred Heart Elementary School to St. Peter's students. This was another of the special blessings that came out of Katrina. An outcome of the devastation of St. Peter's school was that in the fall of 2005, Sacred Heart Elementary School integrated for the first time. God made a way out of no way. It was a smooth transition, thank God. St. Peter's students excelled academically and in sports. Father Mike and the principal were delighted with the decision to integrate the school. The Federal Emergency Management Agency gave the money allocated for the restoration of St. Peter's Elementary School to Sacred Heart School for the construction of a gym and classrooms.

After about ten months, we had collected $200,000 dollars in contributions. Many people had seen the destruction of our church on television and were moved with compassion. Friends of mine from around the country also made contributions and raised funds for the parish.

Rebuilding Structures and Community

I was now ready to move forward with building a new church. I called Fr. Michael Thompson from St. Francis Xavier Church in Baton Rouge and requested his assistance. I was told that he had architectural skills which I could use in the design of a new church. He agreed to draw a sketch for a proposed new church that I could present which would be refined later by my parishioners. I was impressed by Father's enthusiasm and love of the Society of St. Joseph and grateful for his help.

After receiving the drawing from Fr. Thompson, I called a parish meeting to discuss construction of the new church and the additional fundraising that would be required. I felt that it would be important for us to demonstrate our ability to be financially self-sufficient by raising the additional funds ourselves. And, knowing the spirit of the parish that I grew up in, I was confident that we could. In the early 1960's when the bishop disapproved of the parish building a new church, the parishioners (who were much less financially stable) had defiantly raised funds to build anyway. They worked hard to do what was needed to make the church a reality. Unfortunately, the parishioners who led that undertaking were now dead.

Most of the current parishioners had good jobs, homes and cars so, embarking on a capital campaign was not an unreasonable expectation. Since most of them lived in Moss Point, right outside of Pascagoula, their homes had not been as impacted by Katrina as those who lived in the city.

St. Peter was no longer a missionary church, nevertheless, I again encountered the "mission church" attitude and expectation of being supported by contributions from the north even though we had already received generous contributions and assistance. For over 100 years, many Caucasian priests working in the south had solicited funds from white Catholics in the north to help with various projects in poor African American Catholic churches. This type of assistance may have been necessary in earlier years, but not now. In addition, as a black pastor, I did not have the same type of resources in the north and most importantly, I felt it was imperative that we begin to assume responsibility for our own church and discontinue acting like a "mission church". The generous contributions from around the country had provided a considerable nest egg which we could use to begin the re-build. Black Protestant churches in the area had no such expectations and no problem building very nice new churches. I felt that if we continued to act as dependents, we would be treated as dependents.

The parishioners who had financially sustained St. Peter for many years did not appreciate my unwillingness to go beg for the necessary additional funds. They stubbornly made the decision not to support me in the effort to rebuild.

Shortly thereafter, I received an offer to purchase St. Joseph the Worker Church in Moss Point which had plans to move and build a church in Vancleave, MS. I thought that this might be an answer to my prayers because many of the parishioners resided in Moss Point. That offer eventually fell through because the price of the property that St. Joseph parish wanted to purchase had increased astronomically after the hurricane. We were again at "square one"---needing to rebuild a church.

My parishioners were adamant about not embarking on a capital campaign to support new construction. I perceived echoes and remnants of: "Who does he think he is? Isn't he the son of Willie and Velma?" I realized that we were at a stalemate and I am not one who can choose to stand still and not move forward in faith. Consequently, I requested a transfer.

From the beginning, my family and friends had been skeptical about my coming to Pascagoula because the history of priests being successful in their home parishes was not positive. In spite of their objections, I went because I wanted very much to make a contribution to the parish that had supported my vocation.

I will never forget the pain that I felt on the Sunday that I told the parishioners that the Mass I was concluding would be my last for St. Peter. I informed them that they would have a new pastor on Friday. One of the Caucasian parishioners of Sacred Heart shouted from the pew that they would accept me as their pastor.

I read my letter to them from the pulpit letting them know the reason for my transfer and that I was leaving $1.6 million in the bank that had come from various sources. I informed them that my new Toyota Prius (which many thought had been purchased with parish funds) was purchased with insurance money which I received when my car was damaged in the hurricane. I wished them success in the construction of the new church and assured them that they would always be in my prayers.

Father Charles McMahon arrived on Friday as the new pastor of St. Peter the Apostle Church. I am told that he reassured the parishioners that he was not coming as their "white messiah". He also assured them that the financial records were in order and all of the church's money was accounted for. Soon after, the parishioners began working with Father to schedule fund raisers to build a new church.

After paying the debt owed to the Diocese of Biloxi that had accumulated over the years, a new multi-purpose facility was built in 2009. It is still being used as the church. The parishioners have now raised sufficient funds to begin construction of a church but Father McMahon informed them that their income is insufficient to sustain four buildings and pay for the exorbitant flood insurance now required. So, they continue to diligently raise funds and pray that the good St. Peter will intercede on their behalf for a new church. They still hope to break ground on a new church in late 2016 on the land once occupied by the school.

―――――― ⚘ ――――――

CHAPTER 14

A Beacon on the Hill

"We've Come This Way by Faith"

FATHER CHIFFRILLER ASSIGNED me to be the pastor of Our Lady of Perpetual Help Parish (OLPH), on the hill in Anacostia, a low-income community in southeast Washington, D.C.   When I arrived, on December 22, 2006, I found a parish family that was divided and broken as a result of a conflict that had been festering among them. The Washington Post, not a friend to Catholicism, was publicizing the conflict as a racial feud between the pastoral staff and the parishioners. In reality, it was a matter of a misuse of church property that had been permitted to go on for too long. Conflict and division had arisen among the parishioners who had taken one side or the other.

During the first four weeks, I took the time to get to the root of the problem and to speak with those involved. I then had a meeting with the key persons causing the conflict. One party readily admitted what he did to cause and fuel the conflict. He graciously apologized to the parishioners. The apology of the first person brought peace to the parish family and stimulated the necessary healing. The other party, who had been functioning in the parish from a position of authority, refused to apologize or admit any culpability. I reclaimed the pastor's authority and no longer allowed him to have a major leadership role in church ministries. As a result of his diminished role, parishioners who had left the parish because of his negative influence, now returned. It fell upon me in liturgical services and meetings with parish organizations to strengthen the unity of our parish family through the celebration of our faith, reconciliation, and love. Gradually, parish unity was restored and celebrated in our Sunday Eucharist.

Our Lady of Perpetual Help Parish took pride in its black heritage and its status in Church history. The church was established in 1920 when Blacks withdrew from the segregated and unwelcoming St. Theresa Church at the bottom of the hill. They went to the top of the hill and built a church with permission of the bishop. "The Hill" is the second highest place in the District of Columbia with an exquisite panoramic view of the city of Washington, D.C. They originally wanted to name the church for Blessed Martin de Porres but were unable to do so because he had not yet been canonized. A large banner of St. Martin de Porres now reverently hangs at the rear of the church. Every year, the parish celebrates an outdoor Mass in June to commemorate their procession out of St. Theresa's Church up to the top of hill where OLPH parish continues to flourish and serve the community.

Once the internal conflict had been resolved, I began developing leadership workshops for the Parish Council members and other leaders of parish organizations. Gradually, the Parish Council began to function effectively as an informed advisor to the pastor.

The gospel choir, founded by Mrs. Lahohnne Alexa Swann, became a strong ministry under the able leadership of Mr. George Stewart. We anxiously looked forward to the celebration of Holy Week which now incorporated African American spirituality. We began with the "Spy Wednesday" Mass. At the liturgy of the Word, we enacted a portion of the play, *"Between Two Thieves"*. Judas, the villain, and all of the characters surrounding him, were highlighted. This play captured the attention of the all the worshippers. They couldn't wait to see what else Father Norvel had up his sleeves.

Holy Thursday began with the Seder Supper, celebrated as closely as possible to the Jewish ritual. During the celebration, I reminded the parishioners of our personal and spiritual history of slavery and our Passover to freedom brought about by Christ our Liberator. The last cup of blessing at the Seder was the point at which Jesus established the Eucharist. A⁺ this time, everyone processed from the Panorama Room in the parish hall to the church where the Associate Pastor, Father Oswald Pierre Pierre-Jules, was waiting to celebrate the Mass of the Last Supper. Our parish ministry to the poor and needy in the community was highlighted and symbolized in the washing of the feet. Nourished and fortified by the Eucharist, the worshippers were sent forth to share their blessings of love and peace in their families and in the community.

The Good Friday service began with a full assembly. During the singing of the Passion, I stopped at "they crucified Him". I solemnly walked to the rear of the church to take up my cross and don a crown of thorns. With theatrical blood splattered over my face, I processed down the center aisle, carrying the cross to the sanctuary. Men dressed as solders whipped me down the aisle. When I fell under the cross, they shouted, "Get up and move along". I slowly made my way to the sanctuary where I fell for the third time with the cross lying on my chest. At this part of the service, the solders asked the parishioners: "If you have sinned, causing the death of this innocent man, come and nail your nail into the cross". Well, you could have heard a pin drop until the first brave soul came forth to nail her nail. Many of the parishioners tapped the nail lightly causing it to fall to the floor. It was retrieved by the solder and given back to the person who was then told hit the nail harder. Many of the men exited the church for a smoke until the nailing was completed. After everyone had put a nail into the cross, the soldiers helped me up, put the cross in a stand, and I continued with the reading of the Passion. Under the cross, I preached the significance of the suffering and death of Jesus our Liberator.

At the end of the Mass, I carried the cross on my shoulder to the street. Everyone marched in silence through the community taking turns carrying the cross. People came out of their homes in awe and respectful reverence, cars stopped as drivers and passengers acknowledged our celebration of Good Friday. When we returned to the church, the cross was firmly affixed on the lawn in front of the church. A red chasuble (robe) was draped on the cross symbolizing Christ's ultimate sacrifice for the redemption of all. Everyone was then asked to depart in a spirit of reverence and gratitude as they prepared for the great day of the resurrection.

During the first two years of my pastorate, I got away with having a sunrise service. It was beautiful on the hilltop but, eventually, we had to follow the liturgical mandate to have the Easter Vigil service instead. Unfortunately, the Church no longer allowed Easter sunrise services. Our Easter Vigil began as usual, with the blessing of the new fire and the solemn procession into the dark church for the singing of the *Exultet,* a hymn before the Easter candle that praises and thanks God for the Light and what it represents: God's saving activity throughout human history and ultimately, Christ's defeat of death and resurrection from the dead. The *Exultet* was sung by Debra Tidwell-Peters, a professional jazz singer. With lighted candles, everyone stood in reverence and heartfelt joy. The Word of God followed liturgically proclaiming the history of our salvation. Instead of the proclamation of creation from the Book of Exodus, I had the lector use Langston Hughes' *"Creation".* You could actually feel reverential tension and joy in the body of each worshipper. The rest of the Easter Vigil was enhanced by the beautiful traditional Easter hymns that are so dear to all of us.

At the conclusion of the Easter Mass on Sunday morning, a beautifully decorated Easter Wagon filled with Easter candy, eggs and gifts was drawn down the aisle of the church to the tune of "The Easter Parade". All of the children and young at heart followed the Easter Wagon to the hill top where an Easter egg hunt was initiated. The children were overwhelmed with joy!

The Panorama Room was known throughout the District of Columbia as the place where the largest parish bingo in the City was held on Friday evenings, where cabarets were frequently held and dances for the teens and adults. Because we couldn't obtain tickets to attend any of the Inaugural Balls for President Barack Obama, I set up the Panorama Room for our very own Inaugural Ball. Parishioners and friends bought tickets and came from all around the Washington area. I was delighted to welcome my three sisters, cousins and friends who came to D.C. for our Inaugural Ball. I hired a band for the occasion and food and wine were served. President Obama missed the finest Inaugural Ball in the City!

My pastoral ministry at OLPH was truly one of the most fruitful parish ministries of my life. I was very happy and felt the guidance and blessings of the Holy Spirit under my wings. Appreciation for my service was frequently acknowledged by the parishioners and I was encouraged to continue on in the Name of the Lord.

During my tenure at OLPH, I had the privilege of expanding or facilitating several church ministries. I approved the establishment of the Unity Health Care Re-Entry Center, a halfway house for former inmates opened in a trailer on our campus. I employed one of the men, Robert Buchanan, a Caucasian, to work in the parish after his release. He is still employed at OLPH and drives each day from a location near Richmond, VA to work in the parish. He is so grateful for the love and support that the parish provided to him in his time of need.

Under my leadership at OLPH, the Women's Ministry was initiated to enhance, facilitate and recognize the contributions of women in the parish. It has grown and continues to minister to women in the parish and the community.

The "Blessing of the City" was also revived during my tenure at OLPH. In a ceremony on top of the hill overlooking Washington, I sprinkled the city with holy water and we all prayed for God's blessings on His people and the federal government. Many people, including Congressional Representatives, came from all over the city to participate.

I allowed the fraternal order of police to use the Panorama Room for their annual Christmas party for children in public schools. They had Santa Claus come in by helicopter with clothes, shoes, coats, bicycles and toys for needy children in the community. Gifts were followed by dinner and a program. As a result of this, the police provided enhanced security for the parish. On the fourth of July, the parish provided food and beverages for the on-duty police patrolling the community who could not be with their families.

We were happy to welcome the Washington School for Girls into the empty classrooms of our elementary school. Having the girls on our campus not only restored life to our school and campus but also provided opportunities for evangelization.

In 2011, during the time the Josephites were preparing for the celebration of its General Chapter meeting, I was acutely aware that the Society needed strong leadership to unify our priests around a single vision, to renew our commitment to fostering vocations at our House of Formation in Nigeria, and to inspire recommitment to our ministry in the African American community. As a committed and loyal son of St. Joseph, I asked those who attended daily Mass at OLPH to pray that our Chapter would be fruitful and that the best man to advance the mission of the Society would be selected as Superior. We prayed fervently, not anticipating what would be the surprising outcome. The parishioners still teasingly remind me of those prayers.

Parish Scenes

S

*St. Benedict the Moor Gospel Choir Washington D.C.
*Photos from Maryknoll magazine, May 1974

*Chatting with Mr. & Mrs. Mahoney
St. Benedict the Moor, Washington, D.C.

St. Marianna and me with two young
boys and my dog, Duke
St. Francis Xavier, Baltimore, ND

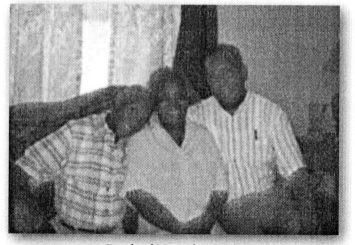

David and Mary Alice James
St. Francis Xavier, Baton Rouge, LA

With Antoinette Planer, Jean Carter, Fannie Joseph
St. Peter the Apostle, Pascagoula, MS

Most Pure Heart of Mary Gospel Choir
Mobile, AL

l

Debra Tidwell-Peters
singing the Exultet
Our Lady of Perpetual Help, D.C.

Millicent Hawkins carries the cross on Good Friday
Our Lady of Perpetual Help, D.C.

Parishioners from St. Isadore in Illinois who
came to help rebuild after Katirna, Pascagoula, MS

Altar Call at St. Brigid
Los Angeles, CA

CHAPTER 15

— ⁂ —

"For Such a Time as This"

"Give Me a Clean Heart"

OUR GENERAL CHAPTER meeting was convened by Father Edward Chiffriller at St. Joseph Seminary. I was an elected delegate to the conference. The Chapter was opened with a Mass of the Holy Spirit seeking guidance and blessings for the election and the decisions to be made. As time for the election approached, I began to concentrate on the names that had been put forth as potential candidates. At the last minute, my name was thrown into the mix of names proposed. This did not concern me because Bishop John Ricard was among those being considered and I was convinced that he would be elected. Four ballots are required to elect a new Superior. At the conclusion of the third ballot, I realized that the number of votes I had was perilously close to those of Bishop Ricard. Though still somewhat confident, I had a growing fear that it was now possible for me to be elected. The fourth ballot was cast and I received three more votes than Bishop John Ricard. Father Edward Chiffriller announced to the assembly that we had elected the first African American Superior General of the Society of St. Joseph of the Sacred Heart in its 140-year history! On June 14, 2015, I became the thirteenth Superior General of the Josephites. There was astounding applause by the delegates as I embarrassingly wiped away my tears and Fr. Chiffriller handed the gavel of the Superior General over to me. The Chapter was temporarily stopped to give me time to select my Vicar. Word of my election went through the Society and the Josephite parishes like wild fire.

To my surprise, my selection of Father Michael Thompson as Vicar General was met with a mixture of surprise and displeasure. He had come to my aid in Pascagoula following Hurricane Katrina and I felt that he would be supportive. Despite their reaction, the assembly confirmed him. Later, many of my former parishioners (who apparently knew more than I did) also expressed dismay at my selection. Father Tom Frank, who had been my student in the diaconate program and my associate at St. Benedict the Moor, was elected Consultor General. I knew him well and I trusted and respected him.

Although being elected Superior General was totally unexpected, after thinking about all of my experiences in parishes north, south, east and west; in national leadership positions within and outside of the Society; in Josephite formation programs for deacons and seminarians; in St. Augustine High School; in pioneering ventures such as Iperu-Remo, St. Benedict the Moor and St. Brigid, I came to believe that God had prepared me "for such a time as this". I had a historical perspective that exceeded fifty years and there was no area of the Josephite ministry and mission that I had not experienced and worked to help develop. With that perspective, I humbly assumed my responsibilities as Superior with a commitment to make a positive difference for our priests and the Society. God is good!

I was really pleased to have received letters of congratulations from most of the bishops in the United States. I have an album full of their letters and those of many religious Superiors, priests and religious sisters congratulating me on my election. I learned later that I was not only the first black Superior of the Josephites, I was the first black priest to serve as Superior General of any religious order in the United States. In his letter of congratulations, retired Cardinal Theodore McCarrick of the Archdiocese of Washington, D.C. declared to me that I was <u>his</u> Superior and that every day when he passed by St. Joseph Seminary on his way to work, he prayed for me and the Josephite mission. It was a special thrill to also receive a letter of congratulations from the first African American President of the United States, Barack Obama! My father would have been very proud.

The General Council worked well with me during the first year. We were carefully putting on the mantel of leadership. There was no manual, no succession plan, and no summary report to provide me with direction or focus. Needless to say, it was a bit intimidating not knowing where to begin or even what questions to ask my Secretary.

As I fumbled along those first few days in an effort to grab hold of the reigns, I was confronted with a monumental problem at St. Augustine High School. A very public and nasty schism developed over the issue of paddling the students. The Board of Trustees and the School Board of St. Augustine were on one side of the issue and the Executive Board and the archdiocese were on the other side. The School Board, Trustees, principal, and parents wanted to continue the practice of paddling even though it was against the law and the mandates of the Archbishop and the Josephite Superior General. We could not convince them that there were more acceptable and effective ways to discipline the students.

There was also a misunderstanding about the authority of the Josephites and the archdiocese to make decisions for the school. For some reason, after fifty-four years of Josephite ownership and administration, certain members of the School Board thought that they could just seize and secularize the school. The Josephites still owned the school however, and were responsible for its administration. The school's Charter required that it could only operate under the auspices of the Josephites and with the approval of the archdiocese.

Because St. Augustine's visibility in the community was very high and the principal had been very defiant, very vocal, and very public, negotiations were very sensitive and crucial. This was the first real test of my leadership. Everyone in New Orleans and St. Aug alumni around the country were watching and waiting for a satisfactory resolution. After a number of very tense meetings and legal maneuverings pursued over a year's time, the principal and several board members were removed and replaced. Members of the Executive Council worked very diligently with me and we were finally able to restore confidence and a level of normalcy. It was a tough first test.

Delegates to the General Council meeting in 2007 had voted to reopen the Josephite house in Iperu-Remo. This meant that we would need a housing facility for Josephite candidates who moved on to study philosophy after the initial period of discernment in Iperu-Remo. I decided early on that making this a reality was one of the primary things I wanted to accomplish during my tenure as Superior General. Establishing the house of study for philosophy students would solidify our program and help ensure that we could train future Josephite candidates from Nigeria. This would ultimately reduce expenses by having the seminarians receive training in Nigeria rather than in the United States.

Under my leadership, the General Council voted to establish the St. Martin de Porres House of Studies. Up to this point, Josephite candidates were being sent to Abuja to study philosophy at the M.S.P. major seminary. Although good, this training was not compatible with the Josephite apostolate to African Americans. After exploring the possibilities, I decided that the new house of studies should be located in Ibadan (only fifty miles from Iperu), rather than Abuja which was 500 miles away. Having the two Josephite houses so close would facilitate community and brotherhood. I explored the cost of building the new house but it was untenable. Fortunately, we were able to rent the Marble Hotel for five years which is less costly and adequate to serve our needs until we are able to build a Josephite complex.

One of the more memorable experiences of my tenure, was a trip to Rome with Bishop John Ricard to meet with Archbishop Savio Tai Fai Hon in order to affirm the Society's approval to continue selecting and training young men in Africa for service as Josephite priests in the United States. It was important to get this affirmation before opening the St. Martin de Porres House of Studies in Nigeria.

The Archbishop politely informed me that he was aware of our house of spiritual formation in Iperu-Remo. He let me know that our strong and positive relationship with the Missionaries of St. Paul, the first foreign missionary community of Nigeria, was key to Rome's approval. He went on to say that I should not hesitate to contact him if I experienced any difficulty. The meeting was warm and cordial.

After the meeting with Archbishop Hon, Bishop Ricard took me on a walking tour of Rome. Although I had been there before, it was wonderful to tour the city with someone who had lived there and who knew so much about the city's history, shrines and architecture.

One of the best decisions that I made as Superior General was to accept Holy Name Parish as the second Josephites parish on the west coast. Holy Name was not in debt and the elementary school was well-operated. In addition, it is less than twenty minutes from St. Brigid Church, the Josephite parish that I pastored in the late 1970's and early 1980's. I was motivated to accept Holy Name because a second parish in Los Angeles would provide companionship for the Josephite pastor at St. Brigid.

I asked Father Stanley Ihuoma, Pastor of All Saints Parish in east New Orleans, to consider being pastor of Holy Name Parish. To my delight, he responded: "If that's what you want, I'll go". His parishioners at All Saints Parish really hated to see him leave, nevertheless, they sent him away with their blessings.

Holy Name Parish welcomed Fr. Stanley with opened arms. They had petitioned me for quite a while to send a Josephite to be their pastor. They rejoiced when their prayers were answered. Father Stanley is doing an outstanding job as pastor of Holy Name. The school children love having him in the classrooms and on the school campus. He has also established a good working relationship with Father Michael Okechukwu, the pastor of St. Brigid Parish.

It was a special privilege as Superior General to welcome my mentor, Father Edward J. Lawlor, to the Josephite Manor (nursing/retirement home) in Baltimore. We celebrated his one hundredth birthday in August of 2013 with a party at the Manor. It was a very happy day and celebration for him. He was very proud and happy that the young boy whom he invited to become a Josephite many years ago, was now his Superior General. At one hundred and one years of age, Father Lawlor went to his eternal reward in heaven. It was my honor to celebrate his funeral Mass and to bury him in the Josephite plot at the New Cathedral Cemetery in Baltimore. May he rest in eternal peace!

During the four years of my administration, I had the pleasure of visiting all of our parishes and the Josephites who staffed them. I was honored to be able to talk with each priest to determine how we, at headquarters, could support them personally and their work in the parishes. It gave me special pleasure to be welcomed by their parishioners and to hear of the great work being done by the Josephites.

Receiving the Promises of our Nigerian seminarians in Temporary and Perpetual membership in the Society was truly the highlight of my tenure as Superior General! It was wonderful to participate in their ordinations and to celebrate this very special occasion with them and their families. The long-awaited and joyful ordinations culminated the first step of their journeys as Josephite priests. It was a special privilege to be able to give them their first parish assignments as Josephite priests.

I felt there was a need to pull the membership together to review the charism and mission of the Society and to give the older priests an opportunity to meet and get to know our new Nigerian priests. I wanted to focus on this during our Convocation so, we selected the theme: "Community as Ministry". Most members of the Society assembled for this meeting at Holy Name Passionist Retreat Center in Houston in June of 2013. The meeting got off to good start however, I was soon blindsided by five Josephites who spearheaded a confrontation and accused me of making decisions they did not agree with. The confrontation came with a fury that knocked the wind out of me. The accusations were harsh, unrelenting, and disrespectful. Several priests felt that I was making decisions without the full consent of the General Council Executive Team. They did not accept that it was completely within my authority as Superior General to make certain independent decisions about the administration of the Society.

They initially objected that I had assigned two new priests as pastors without seeking approval of the General Council Executive Team.

They were also displeased that I had referred a Nigerian seminarian who had been dismissed from the M.S.P.'s to be assessed by our formation program for admittance into the Josephite formation program. I had been asked by a M.S.P. priest to assess and consider the particular candidate in question whom he felt had been unjustly dismissed from their community. Some of the young Nigerian priests mistakenly believed that I was endorsing and expediting this young man through the admission process. The truth was that I did not make a decision about the candidate's qualifications, I appropriately referred him to the Josephite formation team for assessment.

Finally, they were upset that I had decided to locate the St. Martin de Porres House of Studies in Ibadan rather than Abuja. I feel that the young priests were resisting any changes in the process they had experienced and had been instigated to protest. The resulting confrontation with me was very disrespectful, set a bad precedence, and was a disservice to the young priests, many of whom were attending their first general meeting and did not fully understand the operations of the Society. In the fifty years that I have been a priest, I have never seen anything like this outburst. Although I wanted to address the objections of my accusers, I didn't. I did not want to add to the discord so, I let them continue to vent. I finally explained the authority of the Superior General to make decisions. At that point, the assembly calmed down a bit but the damage had been done.

50TH Anniversary of Priesthood

In January of 2015, my sisters, friends, and I began preparing for the celebration of my Fiftieth Anniversary of Ordination to the Priesthood on March 27th.

Many invitations were sent announcing my Jubilee celebrations scheduled for March 21st at St. Anthony's Church in Atlanta, March 27th in Pascagoula and May 1th in Washington, D.C. with other Josephites celebrating milestone anniversaries in 2015.

The Atlanta celebration was a trifecta! In addition to my 50th anniversary, we also celebrated Kirt's, seventy-fifth birthday, and Paulette and Marion's twenty-fifth wedding anniversary. What a joyous celebration this was for our family! We welcomed guests from Nigeria: Monsignor Valentine Awoyemi (Diocese of Ijebu-Ode), Fr. Albert Adeleke, Josephine Joseph and Eddie Onah. Unfortunately, Godwin Urama was not able to get a visa to come. We were both very disappointed.

The Atlanta celebration began with a "Family and Friends" fish fry on Friday evening at Paulette and Marion's home. I offered a Mass of Thanksgiving on Saturday morning which was concelebrated by the President of the National Black Catholic Clergy Caucus, Fr. Kenneth Taylor; Fr. Jeffery Ott, pastor of Our Lady of Lourdes in Atlanta; Fr. Giles Conwill, longtime friend and a priest in the Archdiocese of Atlanta; Fr. Kenneth Westray (Archdiocese of San Francisco); Fr. Michael Okechukwu, the wonderful homilist (one of the young Nigerian men that I trained) and pastor of St. Brigid in Los Angeles; Monsignor Edward Branch, Director of the Catholic Center at Atlanta University Center; and, Fr. Victor Galier, Pastor of St. Anthony Catholic Church where the anniversary Mass was celebrated. Many of Paulette and Marion's friends came from around the country along with Marion's father, siblings, children and several other relatives. His uncles Joe and Rene' played their saxophones at the Mass and reception. Several of our Norvel cousins: Ivrion, Robert, Paul and Evelyn also came from Pascagoula to be with us. After the Mass, we enjoyed a delicious luncheon in the atrium of Morehouse School of Medicine at Atlanta University Center. It was a wonderful celebration!

Longtime friends, Sisters Marianna Halsmer, Lois Davis, Patsy Guyton, Clementina Givens, Josephine Joseph and Eddie Onah attended both the Atlanta and Pascagoula celebrations. Sisters Clementina and Patsy could not travel to the Pascagoula celebration but Sister Charlotte Marshall joined us there.

Sister Lois, Josephine, Eddie and I drove to New Orleans to attend the Episcopal Ordination of Fr. Fernand Cheri, O.F.M. at the Basilica of St. Louis three days before my anniversary. We arrived just in time for me to join the entrance procession of the clergy. Within the Basilica we were surrounded by the glorious voices of the African American Gospel Mass Choir singing under the direction of the Bishop Elect's brother, Richard Cheri.

The historical ordination went smoothly and in keeping with the pomp and circumstance of the Roman Catholic Church tradition until we came to the end of the Mass at which time Bishop Cheri sang and danced in the sanctuary! This bold and joyful display heralded a new episcopal era for the church of New Orleans!

As I sat in the Cathedral during the Episcopal Ordination, I could not help but recall the joy of my own ordination there fifty years ago. I thanked my Good Shepherd profoundly for calling me to the priesthood and for the amazing and fulfilling journey of my vocation. What a blessing it was to be there at that moment in humble gratitude for the rich blessings God has showered upon me throughout my pastoral ministry. I am convinced that God can bless and do much with very little. He demonstrated this with the loaves and the fishes, he demonstrates this every time the Mass is celebrated and he has demonstrated this in my life. I am deeply grateful for all He has done with and through me for the building and glory of His kingdom!

On the 27th of March, my Jubilee celebration reached its peak with the Anniversary Mass celebration at Sacred Heart Church in Pascagoula. Bishop Roger Morin, Ordinary of the Diocese of Biloxi, and ninety-two year old, Bishop Joseph Howze, Bishop Emeritus of Biloxi, were both present and offered words of congratulations at the end of Mass. Mrs. Carolyn Smoke from Mobile played the piano and directed the choir composed of choir members from St.

Peter and Heart of Mary in Mobile. My brother Knights of Peter Claver supported me at both the Atlanta and Pascagoula celebrations.

Father Kenneth Brown, whom I taught at St. Augustine High School, delivered an outstanding homily. When he was at St. Aug, I anticipated his call to the priesthood. His homily indicated that he knew a bit about me as well. Unfortunately, Father Kenneth died suddenly of a brain aneurism less than a month later. I celebrated his funeral Mass at Xavier University Chapel in New Orleans.

The anniversary Mass was followed by a reception and banquet in Sacred Heart's parish hall which had been beautifully decorated by Carolyn and the host committee. Guests included friends and parishioners from virtually all of the parishes that I had served over the years. Dr. Todd Coulter served as Master of Ceremony for the evening. Joseph Lewis (Marion's uncle) and his band provided music and Father Oswald P. Pierre Jules, my former Associate at Our Lady of Perpetual Help Parish, was the guest speaker. A good time was had by all. I am grateful to my sister, Carolyn, who organized and co-chaired the celebration with Gwen Lewis, Marion's aunt from Mobile. Other women from St. Peter organized the Mass logistics and served as Eucharistic ministers, hosted the reception, decorated the hall, helped with the invitations and sold ads for the souvenir program booklet. Donna and Millicent Hawkins, who came from OLPH in Washington, D.C to be with us, also offered invaluable assistance setting up and helping things to go smoothly. My sister, Paulette, also helped with the invitations and the Mass and souvenir program booklets. I am profoundly grateful to each of them especially Carolyn, whom I commend in prayer to God's love and mercy.

The anniversary events concluded on May 1st, the Feast of St. Joseph the Worker, at Our Lady of Perpetual Help Parish in Washington, D.C. It was my honor as Superior General to offer the Mass of Thanksgiving with the other Josephites who were in D.C. to celebrate their milestone anniversaries: Fathers Joseph Calamari, Walter Cerbin, Edward Mallowney, and Howard Byrd. The church was filled with well-wishers, friends, Josephites and other priests, religious brothers and sisters. I was happy to have my sisters there to celebrate with me. My former parishioners of OLPH went out of their way to make this an outstanding celebration. A luncheon followed the Mass. The Panorama Room was beautifully decorated and the food was delicious. OLPH parishioners did everything possible to make their former pastor happy and to make all of the guests feel welcomed. It was a special joy to be able to celebrate my 50th priestly anniversary as Superior General of the Josephites!

CHAPTER 16

—— ✣ ——

"He's Never Failed Me Yet"

My term as Josephite Superior General was rapidly coming to an end.

Fathers Thompson and Tom Frank made preparations for the General Conference which was scheduled for June 15, 2015 at St. Joseph Seminary. Newly ordained, Bishop Fernand Cheri, opened the Conference with a Mass and reminded us of the great work the Josephites have done throughout the country, especially in New Orleans where his life was touched by them. He advised us to renew our ministry to African Americans and be reminded of that ministry during the days of our Chapter meeting.

After the delegates were verified and ballot counters were confirmed, the election began. Meeting rules require that there be four ballots. The first three went smoothly with me leading by two votes. On the fourth ballot, the votes for Fr. Thompson exceeded those for me by two. On June 16, 2015, Fr. Michael Thompson became the new Superior General of the Society of St. Joseph. Word, again, spread like wildfire through the community and some of our Josephite parishes.

After the election, I read a letter to the delegates which I had written three months earlier in anticipation of this outcome. I thanked the priests for giving me the privilege and honor of serving the Society as Superior General. I affirmed that I had served the Society faithfully and would be forever grateful for that privilege. I then requested a month's vacation and permission to take a spiritual sabbatical. I had not taken a sabbatical in the fifty years of my priesthood. After reading my letter, I immediately turned the gavel over to Father Thompson. I remained at the Chapter for another day and a half. On the third day, I opted to leave and return to Headquarters to begin packing.

Paulette came to help me gather and pack up my possessions to ship to Atlanta. Although I got rid of a lot of things, I still had my bicycle and fifty boxes reflecting fifty years of teaching, preaching, books, awards, photographs, family mementos and other memorabilia from Nigeria and the parishes I had served. The collection included a Resolution from Mayor Bradley from my time at St. Brigid; the Brother Joseph Davis Award, the highest award from the National Black Clergy Caucus; a throw with the names of my family members (a gift from one of my parishioners); a hand-carved nativity set from Nigeria; a framed letter from President Obama; photos albums soiled during Hurricane Katrina; bookends that were given to me at my ordination; a porcelain bust of the Virgin Mary (a gift from my parents); and boxes of vestments, sermons, books and photograph albums. I have always loved taking pictures and still carry a camera with me almost everywhere I go. Each item and photograph that I packed captured treasured memories of people, places and experiences over the more than fifty years that I have been in religious life. It was an emotional and exhausting endeavor.

On the morning of July 13, 2015, I got into my Prius and made the twelve-hour drive to Atlanta to live with my sister, Kirt, until beginning my sabbatical in October. I am grateful for the support and reassurance that my family provided during this difficult time. They reminded me that my life and ministry have always been blessed and that He has not brought me this far to leave me.

I had been informed of the pre-election maneuverings almost a year prior to the elections and was warned that if I didn't participate in the "politics", I could anticipate not being re-elected. I was also told "your enemies are under your roof". Prior to the Chapter, several former parishioners also alerted me to what was being planned. When I went to one of our parishes two days before the election, I was approached by one of the parishioners who was very angry. He had heard that members of the Society were planning to have me ousted. I consoled him and told him that it was in God's hands. Months before, I had already let my sisters know what I suspected so that they would not be blindsided by the election results.

Over the summer, I learned more and more (from individuals in and outside of the Society) about the details of what some called the Josephite election "coup".

Unfortunately, it was also discussed in some of our parishes and among the Black clergy around the country. A number of people expressed their anger to me. They could not believe what had happened or how it happened. It was a profoundly hurtful experience. At this point, I didn't know what the future would hold but I did know Who held the future.

As I continued to reflect on the election and the maneuverings leading up to it, I accepted that, through this experience, I was participating in God's Paschal Mystery—life, death, resurrection. The history of the Church and Christianity is full of examples of this mystery; not the least of which is that of our Paschal Lamb. This was not my first experience of being painfully molded in the creative and loving hands of the Potter and, it may not be the last. Each time in the past, God has lifted me to a new awareness or to new emotional and spiritual heights. Through prayer, I was assured that new life (for me and for the Josephites) would be the ultimate outcome and I prayed that I could continue to open my heart and mind, in love and forgiveness, to this probability. "He's never failed me yet."

"I will sing of God's mercy
Every day, every hour
He gives me power.

I will sing and give thanks to Thee
For all the dangers, toils and snares
That He has brought me out.

He is my God and I'll serve Him
No matter what the test
Trust and never doubt
Jesus will surely bring you out
He's never failed me yet."

In August of 2015, I returned to Washington by way of Baltimore to officiate at Sister Clementina Givens' seventy-fifth anniversary of profession to religious life. It was a joyous celebration with Mass and a reception honoring a great religious Sister and educator. Her life has been one of great love, sacrifice and commitment. She is another example of a person who, in her life as a religious, has participated in the Paschal Mystery and has emerged with renewed joy and purpose. She worked full-time until her retirement at the age of ninety-six in the spring of 2016.

Through the Years

With six new Nigerian Josephites

Father Edward J. Lawlor at age 100

With Sr. Lois Davis and Fr. Kenneth Brown

Left: With Mom and Dad at St. Peter in Pascagoula

Right: Mom meets her sister, Mable for the first time in Los Angeles, 1982

Norvel cousins: Carolyn, Kirt, Ivrion, Paulette
Marion, Robert, Evelyn, and me

With Sr. Marianna 2015

My 50th anniversary Mass in Pascagoula with
Bishops Joseph Howze and Roger Morin

CHAPTER 17

"A Time to Mend..."

"Center of My Joy"

IN LATE OCTOBER of 2015, I began a six-week sabbatical at the Canossian Spirituality Center, in Albuquerque, New Mexico. The Center is situated on a beautiful compound conducive to prayer and communication with God through nature. My sabbatical classmates were eight religious sisters. I was the only male among eight religious sisters who hailed from Canada, Hong Kong, Namibia, Ireland, Massachusetts, Pennsylvania and Ohio. They cheerfully greeted me with: "blessed art thou among women". My days there were filled with revelations and affirmations of the Holy Spirit in my life.

We had wonderful and enriching presentations on contemplative prayer by the renowned Father Richard Rohr and other profound presentations by theologians and religious philosophers. There was ample time for prayer and reflection. It was a time to heal...a time to forgive...a time to strengthen my relationship with my Lord and savior. Through the sanctifying grace of the Holy Spirit, I was again able to echo in my heart, the words of St. Augustine: "We are Easter people and Halleluiah is our song!"

Toward the end of our sabbatical, we went on several recreational outings to enjoy the beauty and wonders of the New Mexico desert, including, a sunrise and sunset, a dance fiesta by the Laguna Indians, and a Hot Air Balloon Fiesta. On October 1st, my 80th birthday was celebrated from morning to evening, ending with a fun-filled party. The Canossian Sisters gave me a gift of a glass enclosed image of St. Josephine Bakhita, one of their canonized Saints and a Patron Saint of the Josephites.

This spiritual experience was indeed an enriching and healing blessing from the Lord! When it ended, I felt renewed, refreshed and refocused on my priestly journey with the Lord. I was ready to live the next chapter of my life. Shortly after returning to Atlanta, I was assigned to be mentor and spiritual director for the next generation of Josephite priests at the St. Martin de Porres House of Studies in Ibadan. I anxiously looked forward to sharing the spiritual journeys of these young men.

On November 1, 2015, immediately after my return from New Mexico, I was very pleased and honored to have been invited to participate in the concluding Mass and banquet celebrating the 95th Anniversary of the founding of Our Lady of Perpetual Help Parish. I was warmly received and welcomed by the parishioners.

I thought that the Golden Jubilee celebrations of my ordination were all completed but, when I returned to Atlanta, I was pleasantly surprised to learn that parishioners of St. Brigid Parish in Los Angeles had scheduled another celebration on November 7, 2015. I celebrated the Mass of Thanksgiving and Fathers Michael Okechukwu, Pastor, and Stanley Ihuoma, Pastor of Holy Name Parish, concelebrated. Bishop William Clark of Our Lady of the Angels Pastoral Region of Los Angeles, preached the homily. I was very proud to have my former students, Fathers Michael and Stanley, at the altar with me.

The Gospel Choir, which I founded in 1980 sang two of my favorite hymns: "Give Me a Clean Heart" and "Order my Steps". Bishop Clark presented me with an impressive plaque congratulating me on my Golden Jubilee. As the Mass began, I was pleasantly surprised to notice that my sister, Carolyn, was sitting in the front pew. I had no idea that she would be there! Friends of mine at St. Brigid had befriended Carolyn over the years and had arranged for her to come. Our cousin, Gerard Nelson and his wife LaTonya, from Palmdale, CA also surprised me with their presence.

The Mass was followed by a delicious banquet at the Proud Bird Restaurant. The program included gifts from each of St. Brigid's ministries. "This is Your Life Father Norvel" was presented by Sister Marianna, Father Michael, Stanley Le Sassier ("Mr. Mardi Gras"), Sister Charlotte Marshall, O.S.P. (who traveled from Baltimore to be there), and Robert Long, (President of the Parish Council). The celebration concluded with a toast and everyone dancing the second line (a traditional celebratory New Orleans strut). It was a long evening filled with many special memories of my pastoral ministry at St. Brigid and a powerful confirmation of God's guidance and support during the four years of my pastorate there.

Sister Marianna made the following comments in my honor:

"It was the summer of 1979 when the staff of St. Brigid Church learned that the Josephites would be taking over our Church. It was a hard decision for Fr. Seymour to let go. However, he told us that the new pastor wished to keep the present staff. For us, that was good news! I liked everything about you and especially the feeling I got of "shape up or ship out"'. The Spirit was moving! You are the miracle that took place at that time on South Western Avenue, in Los Angeles, our first African American priest and pastor. All heaven broke loose! In the words of parishioner, Fred Morrero (Rip), "A priest with vision and a proven plan for parish renewal, inculcated the black culture into the liturgical celebration, and the rebirth of the parish began." You started the first Catholic gospel choir in the city. The gifts and talents of the congregation came forth and community outreach programs were established. We had programs for parishioners from the cradle to the grave. Folks were taking pride in their identity. Their quality of life was being improved, and they were being empowered. I saw a camaraderie of people that speak of home! The Gospel choir drew folks from many areas in and outside the parish. Our church was bursting at the seams!

Audio tapes were made of the Gospel Mass. I remember visiting a woman who lived in an apartment several blocks from the church. She was slowly dying of cancer. She had a tape of one of our Masses which she played over and over. She said that it kept her alive, and brought life to her neighborhood. It was a renewal for me as well. No group has shaped my life more than the African American community. Marian Fussey who was on our staff was a significant role model.

Father Norvel, you opened up a whole new world for me. After completing your term for your Community as Consultor General, I accepted your invitation to again work with you as Pastoral Minister at Most Pure Heart of Mary Church in Mobile, Alabama with great joy.

Following four years there, we were assigned to St. Francis Xavier Parish, in Baton Rouge, LA for five years, and Baltimore, the Mother Church of African Americans. Every parish we went to YOU brought a REBIRTH. You and your family were very good to me. Being far away from my own Community, Sisters of Social Service, on the West Coast, I became a part of the Norvel Clan. As I reminisce over the years I spent working with you as Pastoral Minister, how Blessed I was. YOU gave Life to my years--more fullness of life than I had ever experienced."

Sister Marianna and I were pastoral partners for 19 years. I could always be assured of her prayers, encouragement and support. She "had my back" and I am profoundly grateful for her love and friendship. I traveled to Encino, CA in May of 2016 to celebrate her 60th anniversary Mass at the Motherhouse of the Sisters of Social Service where she lives. Sister Marianna is now 92 years young. She still worships at St. Brigid whenever she can. In March of 2015, she traveled to Atlanta and Mississippi to celebrate the 50th anniversary of my priesthood with my family and me. She considers herself, as we do also, a member of the Norvel family.

CHAPTER 18

The Next Chapter

"God Never Fails"

I ARRIVED IN Ibadan on November 18, 2015. The seminarians welcomed me warmly and went out of their way to make sure that I was comfortably situated in my room. The Rector, Father Nixon Mullah, had worked hard to prepare the suite for my arrival.

It was obvious that Father Nixon had also worked hard to convert the Marble Hotel into the Josephite House of Studies for our seventeen seminarians who were studying philosophy at the Dominican Institute. The lawn was beautifully manicured and the rooms were clean and readied for guests. The chapel was also clean and welcoming as a place of prayer.

I was anxious to begin work so I immediately informed the seminarians that I was available to work with them on their spiritual development. During the course of four months, each of them came to initiate individual sessions and discuss their spiritual journey to the priesthood. It was a blessing to have an opportunity to get to know them and to begin learning about their spiritual lives, their studies, their family experiences and their lives at the House of Studies.

The spiritual formation program required only an hour or two in the evenings however, even this was, more often than not, too difficult to fit into their schedules. After Mass each day at 6 a.m., the seminarians were off to school until 1:30 p.m. After lunch, there was a nap, work chores or recreation and then study. Each seminarian was taking eight or nine courses each. Remarkable, they had no text books. They worked from their notes and the notes of their professors. They had to go to the library to access text books. In spite of these difficult circumstances, they were excellent students and generally "A" students. Because of their work loads, there was very little time to sit and talk with them, to schedule programs, or to relax with them. Their studies were intense and their noses were always in the books.

Because Father Nixon did not need or welcome my assistance in other areas of the household administration, I spent ten and a half hours during the day doing nothing productive. Of course I read, prayed and corresponded with loved ones but I am a people-person and have always been very active. I could not continue to remain idle during the day. During the Christmas holidays when the seminarians went home, I remained at the House of Studies alone--unable to leave the compound because I had no means of transportation.

The happiest experience I had at the House of Studies was the celebration of the Solemnity of St. Joseph on March 19th. I was privileged to be the celebrant and homilist for the Mass. At the end of Mass, Father Nixon asked me to share the history of our Society with our guests. Everyone found the history fascinating and had many questions at the conclusion of my remarks. After the talk, a seminarian from another religious community asked me what he needed to do to become a Josephite.

I had just begun to bond with the seminarians when Father Nixon and I decided that the spiritual development program I was developing was not compatible with what he had planned to implement for them. We agreed that I should return to the States.

My brief experience with our seminarians in Ibadan was delightful and fulfilling. It was a painful departure because of the bond that I had been able to create with them and because I would not be able to continue sharing their spiritual journey through their entrance to St. Joseph Seminary, in Washington,

D.C. I appreciate having had this brief opportunity to get to know them. I know it was the best decision.

I returned to Atlanta from Nigeria on March 22, 2016 and immediately submitted my letter of resignation to the Superior General. I spoke with him two weeks later and, on June 5th, I received a letter accepting my retirement. He wished me "many days of rest, good health, and God's grace" and thanked me for my "contributions to the Society and the Church". I will be moving back to D.C. to reside at St. Luke's church with Fr. Cornelius Ejiogu, the pastor. I will be available to serve when help is needed in any of our Josephite parishes.

Though my days as a pastor are apparently over, I am acutely aware that there is still much to be done by the Josephites in the African American community. I am concerned about the education of Black youth, the decline of Black families, violence against and within the Black community, high unemployment (especially among Black youth), and, the inordinate incarceration of Black men. It is difficult to feed a person's soul when her body is hungry. In this land of hope, opportunity, and plenty, many of our brothers and sisters remain among "the least of these".

The Josephites apostolate is needed now, more than ever. Like our founding fathers, we must continue to address the needs of the whole person. To paraphrase Dr. Martin Luther King, Jr., we must not only feed our brothers and sisters, we must courageously address the social and economic policies that leave them on the "Jericho road". This will require vision, commitment and courage. The young Josephites who are now in the vineyard will have their hands full. With prayer, God's grace, and a strong commitment to and love for God's people, I am convinced that they will be able to seize the legacy of our founders and advance the Josephite mission to evangelize and serve the African American community. When our founding fathers came from England as missionaries to start the Josephites, they were required to make an oath to the Superior General to be "father and servant of the Negroes". They further vowed never to commit themselves any other ministry that would cause them to abandon or in any way neglect the special care of the Negroes. I remain ready to do all that I can to help this next generation of Josephites fulfill this noble mission.

I have now been a priest for fifty-one years and I am eighty years old—some would say eighty years young. I still drive with no problem, ride my bicycle as frequently as I can, walk well, enjoy music (opera, classical, jazz, gospel), reading, theater, and traveling. I enjoy talking and visiting with family and friends (mostly former parishioners) from around the country and in Africa. Most importantly, I am still as pleased to be a priest today as I was on March 27, 1965. Great has been His faithfulness!

I have traveled the United States and the world (Jamaica, Spain, Kenya, Cote d'Ivoire, Ghana, Italy, Mexico, Canada, England, the Holy Land, and Nigeria). I have worked with many extraordinary Christian people. I have offered Mass on Mt. Olive and renewed my baptismal vows in the River Jordan. I have met or heard many historic figures speak and/or perform including: Mrs. Coretta Scott King, Dr. Dorothy Height, Pope John Paul, II, President Barack Obama, President Bill Clinton, Ambassador Andrew Young, Secretary Alexis Herman, Nelson and Winnie Mandela, Nat King Cole, Sarah Vaughn and many others.

I was blessed with wonderful parents, a loving family, and a strong faith! My life has been rewarding, challenging, enriching, adventurous and fulfilling. I am a respected leader and elder among Black Catholic clergy and a pioneer of gospel music in the Catholic Church. I pray that my contributions as a pastor and as a priest have served the Catholic Church, the Society of St. Joseph, God's holy people and, most of all, have glorified God's name.

I left nothing on the table and I couldn't ask for more! To borrow the name of Maya Angelou's book, "I wouldn't take nothing for my journey now"! The words of a song by the same name written by Charles Goodman and Jimmie Davis, summarize my sentiments about my remarkable journey.

I wouldn't take nothing for my journey now,
I've got to make it to Heaven somehow.
Though the devil tempts and tries to turn me around.
He's offered everything that's got a name
All the wealth I want and worldly fame,
But if I could, still I wouldn't take nothing for my journey now.
I started out traveling for the Lord many years ago,
I've had a lot of heartaches, had a lot of troubles and woes.
Oh, when I would stumble, then I would humble down.
I'd say, "Thank the Lord, I wouldn't take nothing for my journey now."
There's nothing in this world that can ever take the place of God's Love,
Silver and gold could never buy His love from above.
When my soul needs healing and I begin feeling His power,
I can say, "Thank the Lord, I wouldn't take nothing for my journey now.
Wouldn't take nothin' for my journey now
Gotta make it to Heaven somehow.

I have given it my all! To God be the glory!

Chapter Themes

CHAPTER I

"I Decided to Make Jesus My Choice"
H. Johnson

Some folk would rather have houses
and land.
Some folk choose silver and gold.
These things they treasure and forget
about their soul;

I've decided to make Jesus my choice.
The road is rough, the going gets
tough,
and the hills are hard to climb,
I've started out a long time ago,
there's no doubt in my mind;
I've decided to make Jesus my choice.

CHAPTER II

"Here I Am Lord"
J. Kilbane

Here I am Lord. Is it I Lord?
I have heard you calling in the night
I will go, Lord

If you lead me
I will hold your people in my heart

I the Lord of snow and rain, I have
born my people's pain
I have wept for love for them, they
turn away
I will break their hearts of stone,
Give them hearts for love alone
I will speak my word to them, whom
shall I send

Here I am Lord. Is it I Lord?
I have heard you calling in the night
I will go, Lord

If you lead me
I will hold your people in my heart

CHAPTER III

"I'm Available to You"
Rev. M. Brunson

You gave me my hands, to reach out
to man

To show him Your love and Your perfect plan
You gave me my ears, I can hear your voice so clear. I can hear the cries of sinners, but can I wipe away their tears.

You gave my voice, to speak Your words
To sing all Your praises, to those who never heard. But with my eyes I see a need for more availability. I see hearts that have been broken, so many people to be free.

Chorus:
Lord, I'm available to you, my will I give to you
I 'll do what you say do, use me Lord. To show someone the way and enable me to say. My storage is empty and I am available to you.

Now I'm giving back to you, all the tools you gave to me.
My hands, my ears, my voice, my eyes, so You can use them as You please. I have emptied out my cup, so that You can fill it up.
Now I'm free, I just want to be more available to You.

Aaah, aaah, aaah, aaah
Aaah, aaah, aaah, aaah

Use me Lord to show someone the way and enable me to say.
My storage is empty and I am available to you
My storage is empty and I am available to you, you you
My storage is empty and I am available to you

CHAPTER IV
"Leaning On the Everlasting Arm"
Showalter and Hoffman

What a fellowship, what a joy divine,
Leaning on the everlasting arms;
What a blessedness, what a peace is mine,
Leaning on the everlasting arms.

Refrain:
Leaning, leaning, safe and secure from all alarms;
Leaning, leaning, leaning on the everlasting arms.
O how sweet to walk in this pilgrim way,
Leaning on the everlasting arms;
O how bright the path grows from day to day,
Leaning on the everlasting arms.

Refrain
What have I to dread, what have I to fear,

Leaning on the everlasting arms;
I have blessed peace with my Lord so
near,
Leaning on the everlasting arms.

CHAPTER V
"Great is Thy Faithfulness"
T. Chisholm

Great is Thy faithfulness, oh God my
Father;
There is no shadow of turning with
Thee;
Thou changest not, Thy compassions,
they fail not;
As Thou hast been, Thou forever wilt
be.

Great is Thy faithfulness! Great is
Thy faithfulness!
Morning by morning new mercies I
see.
All I have needed Thy hand hath
provided;
Great is Thy faithfulness, Lord, unto
me!

Summer and winter and springtime
and harvest,
Sun, moon, and stars in their courses
above
Join with all nature in manifold
witness

to Thy great faithfulness, mercy and
love.

Pardon for sin and a peace that
endureth
Thine own dear presence to cheer
and to guide;
Strength for today and bright hope
for tomorrow,
Blessings all mine, with ten thousand
beside!

Great is Thy faithfulness! Great is
Thy faithfulness!
Morning by morning new mercies I
see.
All I have needed Thy hand hath
provided;
Great is Thy faithfulness,
Great is Thy faithfulness,
Great is Thy faithfulness, Lord, unto
me!

CHAPTER VI
"Order My Steps"
D. McClurkin

Order my steps in your word dear
Lord
Lead me guide me everyday
Send your anointing father I pray
Order my steps in your word
Please, order my steps in your word

Humbly I ask thee teach me your will
While you are working help me be
still
Satan is busy God is real
Order my steps in your word
Please, order my steps in your word

Bridle my tongue let my words edify
Let the words of my mouth be ac-
ceptable in thy sight
Take charge of my thoughts both day
and night
Please order my steps in your word
Please order my steps in your word
I want to walk worthy (pause) my
calling to fulfill
Please order my steps Lord-----and
I'll do your blessed will
The world is ever changing (pause)
but you are still the same
If you order my steps (pause) I'll
praise your name

Order my steps (pause) in your word
Order my tongue (pause) in your
word
Guide my feet (pause) in your word
Wash my heart (pause) in your word
Show me how to walk (pause) in your
word
Show me how to talk (pause) in your
word

When I need a brand new song to
sing
Show me how to let your praises ring

CHAPTER VII
"He's Blessing Me"
N. Garner

He's blessing me
Over and over again
He's blessing me
Right here where I stand
Every time I turn around He's mak-
ing a way somehow
Over and over again.
He's blessing me.
He's blessing me (He's blessing me)
Over (over and over again)

The Lord is (He's blessing me) right
here (right here where I stand)
Every time (Every time I turn around
He's making a way somehow)
Over (over and over again)
He's (He's blessing me)

The Lord is blessing, blessing me
right now
The Lord is blessing me He's making
a way somehow
You may not be able to see
Just what the Lord is doing for me

But Over and over again
He's blessing me.
He's in my walk
Oh yes, the Lord is blessing me
He's in my talk,
Oh yes, the Lord is blessing me
He's in my heart and soul,

CHAPTER XVIII

"He's An On Time God"
D. Peoples

He's an on time God,
Yes He is,
He's an on time God,
Yes He is.
He may not come when you want
Him,
But He'll be there right on time.
He's an on time God,
Yes He is.

Just ask the children of Israel trapped
at the Red Sea by the mean ole pharaoh and his army. They had water
all around them and pharaoh on their
backs, but from out of nowhere, God
stepped in and put a highway just like
that.

You can ask the 5,000 hungry souls
he fed on the banks of the river with

2 fishes and 5 loaves of bread. What a
miracle He performed on that multi-
tude, but what he did way back then,
He can do today for me and you.

He's an on time God,
Yes He is,
He's an on time God,
Yes He is.
He may not come when you want
Him,
But He'll be there right on time.
He's an on time God,
Yes He is.

CHAPTER IX

"His Eye is on the Sparrow"
J. Colter

Why should I feel discouraged, why
should the shadows come
Why should my heart fell lonely and
long for Heaven and home
When Jesus is my portion, a constant
friend is He
His eye is on the sparrow and I know
He watches over me
His eye is on the sparrow and I know
He watches me

I sing because I'm happy, I sing because I'm free

His eye is on the sparrow and I know
He watches me, He watches me
His eye is on the sparrow and I know
He watches
I know He watches, I know He
watches me

I sing because I'm happy, I sing because I'm free
His eye is on the sparrow and I know
he watches me, He watches me
His eye is on the sparrow and I know
he watches me, He watches me
He watches me, I never thought, He
watches me

His eye is on the sparrow and I know
he watches me, He watches me
He watches me, I never thought, He
watches me

CHAPTER X

"This Little Light of Mine"
A.B. Christiansen

This little light of mine
I'm going to let it shine
Oh, this little light of mine
I'm going to let it shine
Hallelujah
This little light of mine
I'm going to let it shine
Let it shine, let it shine, let it shine

Ev'ry where I go
I'm going to let it shine
Oh, ev'ry where I go
I'm going to let it shine
Hallelujah
Ev'ry where I go
I'm going to let it shine
Let it shine, let it shine, let it shine

All in my house
I'm going to let it shine
Oh, all in my house
I'm going to let it shine
Hallelujah
All in my house
I'm going to let it shine
Let it shine, let it shine, let it shine

CHAPTER XI

"Blessed Assurance"
F. Crosby

Blessed assurance, Jesus is mine!
Oh, what a foretaste of glory divine!
Heir of salvation, purchase of God,
Born of His Spirit, washed in His
blood. Refrain:
This is my story, this is my song,
Praising my Savior all the day long;
This is my story, this is my song,
Praising my Savior all the day long.

Perfect submission, perfect delight,

Visions of rapture now burst on my
sight;
Angels, descending, bring from
above
Echoes of mercy, whispers of love.
Perfect submission, all is at rest,
I in my Savior am happy and blest,
Watching and waiting, looking above,
Filled with His goodness, lost in His
love.

CHAPTER XII

"In Christ There is No East or West"
J. Oxenham

In Christ there is no east or west,
in him no south or north,
but one great fellowship of love
throughout the whole wide earth.

In Christ shall true hearts
everywhere
their high communion find;
his service is the golden cord
close-binding humankind.

Join hands, disciples of the faith,
whate'er your race may be.

All children of the living God
are surely kin to me.

In Christ now meet both east and
west;
in him meet south and north.
All Christly souls are one in him
throughout the whole wide earth.

CHAPTER XIII

"Lord Help Me to Hold Out"
J. Cleveland

Lord, help me to hold out (3X)
Until my change come

My way may not easy
You did not say that it would be
But when it gets dark
I can't see my way
You told me to put my trust in Thee
That's why I'm asking you

CHAPTER XIV

"We've Come This Far by Faith"
C. Pearson

Chorus
We've come this far by faith
Leaning on the LORD
Trusting in His Holy Word
He never failed me yet
Oh' can't turn around
We've come this far by faith

Don't be discouraged
when troubles is in your life
He will bear your burdens oh
He will remove all our misery and
strife
And that's why
Just the other day
I heard a man say
He didn't believe in God words
But I can truly say I'm a living wit-
ness today
And God has never failed me yet

CHAPTER XV

"Give Me A Clean Heart"
M. Douroux

Give me a clean heart
To see You like I should, hey
To walk the path that's right
To do the thing You would
Give me a clean heart and I will serve
nobody, but You

Give me a clean heart
To lose the double mind
To believe You when You tell me
Everything will be just fine
Just lay Your hands on me Lord
And I will be brand new
And I am calling out to You for a
strength exchange

I will gladly take Your joy for my
weakness
Give me a clean heart and I will serve
nobody, but You
(Give me a clean heart and I will
serve nobody but You)
{Hey, yeah let the band play for two
now, come on now}

Give me a clean heart
A better one I pray
To stay on the path You've chosen
And stick with it all the way
Give me a clean heart and I will serve
nobody, but You

CHAPTER XVI

"He's Never Failed Me Yet"
R. Ray

Trust and never doubt
Jesus will surely bring you out
He never failed me yet

I will sing of God's mercy
Every day every hour
He gives me power
I will sing And give thanks to Thee
For all the dangers, toils & snares
That He has brought me out

He is my God And I'll serve Him
No matter what the test

Trust and never doubt
Jesus will surely bring you out
He never failed me yet

I know God is able
To deliver in time of storm
I know that He'll keep you
Safe from all earthly harm

One day when my weary soul is at
rest
I'm going home to be forever blessed

Trust and never doubt
Jesus will surely bring you out
He never failed me yet

CHAPTER XVII

"Center of My Joy"
R. Smallwood

Jesus, You're the center of my joy,
all that's good and perfect comes
from You.
You're the heart of my contentment,
hope for all I do;
Jesus, You're the center of my joy.

When I've lost my direction, You're
the compass for my way,
You're the fire and light when nights
are long and cold.

In sadness, You are the laughter, that
shatters all my fears,
when I'm all alone, Your hand is
there to hold.

You are why I find pleasure in the
simple things in life,
You're the music in the meadows and
the streams.
The voices of the children, my family, and my home,
You're the source and finish of my
highest dreams.

Jesus, You're the center of my joy,
all that's good and perfect comes
from You.
You're the heart of my contentment,
hope for all I do...

Jesus, You are the center of my joy.
Jesus, You are the center of my joy,
joy, joy, of my joy.

CHAPTER XVIII

"God Never Fails"
C. Nicks

God never fails, God never fails
He abides in me
He gives me victory
For God never fails
You just keep the faith

and never cease to pray
Walk upright, Call Him day noon or
night
He'll be there
There's no need to worry
For God never fails

I never worry
I never fret
Because God almighty
Has never failed me yet
Rebuke and scorn
You know I been reborn
For God never fails

No need to cry
I'm not afraid to die
I got my Lord
I know He's by my side
Daily I trust Him
Never shall I doubt Him
For God never fails